AN AMERICAN SPEAKS OUT
ENOUGH IS ENOUGH

N. E. PARKS

AuthorHouse™
1663 Liberty Drive
Bloomington, IN 47403
www.authorhouse.com
Phone: 1 (800) 839-8640

© *2015 N. E. Parks. All rights reserved.*

No part of this book may be reproduced, stored in a retrieval system, or transmitted by any means without the written permission of the author.

Published by AuthorHouse 04/16/2015

ISBN: 978-1-5049-0167-3 (sc)
ISBN: 978-1-5049-0166-6 (e)

Library of Congress Control Number: 2015904371

Print information available on the last page.

Any people depicted in stock imagery provided by Thinkstock are models, and such images are being used for illustrative purposes only.
Certain stock imagery © Thinkstock.

This book is printed on acid-free paper.

Because of the dynamic nature of the Internet, any web addresses or links contained in this book may have changed since publication and may no longer be valid. The views expressed in this work are solely those of the author and do not necessarily reflect the views of the publisher, and the publisher hereby disclaims any responsibility for them.

CONTENTS

Prologue xiii

Now It's Personal xiii

Introduction xxiii

What Has Gone Wrong In America? xxiii

Chapter One: The Domestic Plan 1

                        Government Policy and Corporate Strategy (Public-Private Partnerships) 4

                        Tax Code Reform 5

                        Energy Independence and Innovation 6

                        Immigration 8

                        Infrastructure Development 10

                        Research and Education 10

                        Climate Change and War 11

Chapter Two: Federal Government Reform 14

                        The United States Presidency 14

The Proliferation of the Federal Government 21

Change the Roles of the Federal Government..........26

Oversight—Follow the Money—

Eliminate Fraud, Waste, and Abuse........................28

Eliminate Duplication of Effort Among

Federal Agencies and Programs...............................36

Change the Federal Budget Process........................38

Office of Personnel Management (OPM)

Guidelines 38

Chapter Three: Congressional Reform 41

Salary and Benefits 47

Campaign Funding Reform......................................49

Lobbying..50

Earmarking Legislation..52

Bicameral Structure of Congress/Term Limits.........54

Electoral College 56

The Two Party System - Make Room for the

Independents and Others...58

Health Care...61

Social Security and Medicare 63

Welfare and Unemployment Reform.......................65

Chapter Four	Where's My White Picket Fence?	70
	The American Dream for Sale	70
	The American Nightmare	73
	Too Big to Fail, Too Big to Prosecute	76
	Federal Reserve System	80
Chapter Five	Life, Liberty, and the Pursuit of Happiness	83
	Taking Back America	92
	American Values	96
	Opportunity	99
	Fairness and Responsibility	101
	Freedom and Security	103
	General Welfare	104
	Paying it Forward	106
About the Author		111

This book is dedicated to our children and grandchildren

A day may come when our nation is measured not by its gross national product or its tallest buildings nor by the accumulation of vast wealth, but by the well-being of its people; by the opportunities to learn and better themselves; by the ability to earn a fair wage; by the safeguards we have in place to take care of those who are in need or disadvantaged; by the integrity of our public officials; and by the fairness of our laws with respect to our governance.

-N.E. Parks

PROLOGUE
NOW IT'S PERSONAL

Our economy in America has been declining over the past several decades and with that went jobs, income levels, pensions, local tax bases, technology and innovation, education, trade skills, and more importantly, the spirit of a free America, a land of opportunity, governed by laws, all of which our nation was founded. And with it we gained trade deficits and budget deficits.

The new American republic established in 1776 was the beginning of a democratic commonwealth that would one day possibly extend to many nations. This new form of government was envisioned by a select few founding fathers, designed to allow for separation of church and state, the emancipation of all people, and established controls on the power of the state. The four page hand written Constitution still serves as a manual to our political framework and the greatest form of government in the world. The forethought found in the document is unbelievable. But it is only as good as the paper it is written on if the principles set forth as the foundation are not practiced and protected by the American people.

The President and Congress establish the rules by which our economy functions and how it directly affects Americans' job opportunities, tax liability, retirement savings, health care and educational opportunities, interest rates, and inflation through the laws enacted, policies and programs implemented, and regulatory practices. Therefore, politics is driving our economy. Unfortunately, the nature of the beast is **reelection**.

If public officials allow lobbyists, campaign funding, big business, and political party caucus and gridlock to drive their decisions or inaction, Americans will be and have been adversely affected in their standard of living and life, liberty, and the pursuit of happiness. Since the Supreme Court has allowed unlimited campaign funding, our only option is to seek out better candidates to run for public office and vote for these candidates, regardless of political party affiliation or amount of campaign funding.

Americans are tired of political games supporting lobbyists and big money policies, they want consensus and action on important national and global issues.

Americans are tired of extreme political parties, finger pointing, and the party caucus system that promotes party unity at the expense of bipartisan consensus and the unity of our nation. They want action directed toward the middle, for the greater good.

Americans are tired of the federal government and Congress managing and passing legislation by crisis. The policies are reactive and not necessarily appropriate, may be vastly more costly, and create more problems.

Americans are tired of government overreach, unaccountability to public responsibility and values, fraud and wasteful overspending of tax payer dollars. Some recent examples are the Internal Revenue System, Veterans Administration, Obamacare, the border crisis, social security disability and welfare fraud, and executive orders that are unconstitutional just to mention a few.

Americans are tired of low and stagnant wages, unemployment/under employment, and raising costs for food, gas, education, and health care.

Americans are tired of job and retirement insecurity caused by outsourcing jobs, creating what looks like to some as corporate greed and un-American values.

Americans are tired of home devaluation and the inability to secure refinanced mortgages with lower interest rates and being subject to fraudulent mortgage loans and home foreclosures while the CEOs and banks that tax payers bailed out are faring well with high incomes, severance packages, and bonuses.

It is time to rethink our political framework and the structure of the federal government. I believe both Congress and the federal government are "too big to function effectively" and have actually been spoiled by excessive spending and excessive funding without accountability or national priorities. We need to take back our government and rethink priorities, policies, and values that are impeding progress toward a larger middle class and a better quality of life for all. The President and Congress can share the blame for not having the work ethic to create alternatives to fix the actual budget and policy problems and focus on policy reform and federal priorities that are impeding our future growth and prosperity as a nation.

It is apparent that politics is standing in the way of adequately serving the American people and making any progress towards change. The arrogance of both branches of government is appalling. Don't forget that the legislative branch is elected by the American people to serve as public servants to the citizens of the U.S. and the executive branch is elected and funded by the American people to carry out federal government missions and foreign policy necessary for the good of the country. Neither should function for self-interest. Over the past 40 years, public policies have helped the wealthy and harmed the less fortunate, forced American businesses overseas, and directly exposing so many average working Americans to such widespread insecurity.

All who are Americans love their country but have not always been proud of it. Land and homesteads were taken from the native Indians by this country. Persons of color were discriminated against and treated inhumanly in all areas of life by this country. Vietnam veterans were not shown the respect and appreciation deserved by Americans as they returned from war. And now the Veterans Administration scandal and fraudulent treatment of our veterans in exchange for senior executive bonuses has set the lower bar of disgust. Then there is the IRS targeting political affiliation, the Benghazi affair in Libya, the Bergdahl swap for five imprisoned terrorist leaders, Obamacare, the border crisis, and the lack of foreign policy with regard to terrorists threatening our country. Enough is enough.

America is not perfect and democracy is an ever evolving state. There is much good about America and her people. We have the ability to change direction when our consciences tell us to, we just need to know what to change. This book is an attempt to highlight many ways the country has fallen out of the people's hands and ways we can get it back on track for the greater good.

We have known for decades that the governmental budget deficits and accumulating debt needed to be addressed to avoid future generations from suffering the ultimate impacts, including selling ownership of our country to other countries. The budget deficit is not the biggest concern for most Americans right now but it does hamper the government's ability to provide adequate programs and services and drives up costs due to interest payments we are paying to borrow money to cover overspending.

The American people are concerned with the revitalization of the economy in the form of jobs for those who want to work and focused fiscal priorities that provide better access to health care and education through lower costs, infrastructure improvement, and other public works. Education and health care costs continue to rise along with increasing unemployment, food prices, and until recently, gas prices. 12 million people were unemployed in 2012, down from 14 million in 2011, taking a toll on families' well-being.

The federal policies and regulations enacted over the years have deterred the growth and sustainability of small business and manufacturing in this country, the practices of big business that outsource jobs overseas for more profits, the greed and corruption of the "too big to fail", "too big to prosecute" financial institutions, the BP oil spill, and the contamination of prescription compound drugs not properly regulated, and the lobbyists and big business that control the politicians and public policy for their financial gain.

Trying to resolve the deficit in the wrong way is having a direct impact on the economy, jobs, and public welfare. There are a lot of moving parts to be analyzed in correcting these problems and they will not be corrected by "sequestration" or any other mindless strategy. It took years, if not decades, to get into this mess. Many policies, programs, and individuals have caused this mess. We must change consciousness to do what is right for the greater good, not for politics, greed, or the status quo.

So what are the lessons of the past and in what direction do we need to head to get Americans back to work, reduce the federal budget deficit, establish national priorities, make Congress functional so it can do its job, make the federal government more effective and efficient, ensure social security and Medicare benefits are available for those who have paid into the programs, address the shortfalls in health care affordability, mental health accessibility, reform the mortgage lending and investment banking practices, support small business, change the tax and trade policies, address the longstanding energy challenge, close our borders and initiate fair immigration policy, modernize the educational system, understand what America's intensions are in the middle east, Russia, and other countries with regard to the current and future conflicts, and support our veterans and the military as they return from war with the many issues they now have to overcome.

The above issues are not new and they continue to worsen the longer we delay in successfully outlining and implementing specific actions that need to be taken to change the policies, programs, and infrastructure that support and contribute to these problems. One must recognize that we cannot legislate ethical behavior or stop personal and corporate greed and corruption. One must also recognize that implementation of these ideas and recommendations will not be possible without clear leadership, collaboration, innovation and bipartisanship. These values and behaviors will have to change if we are ever truly going to rethink the American Dream. These issues have become personal to most Americans, affecting their ability to live, prosper and meet basic needs.

However, the Statue of Liberty, a gift to the United States from the people of France, still stands in America. The statue represents the Roman goddess of freedom, upon it is inscribed the date of the American Declaration of Independence, July 4, 1776. It is an icon of freedom and of the United States.

INTRODUCTION

WHAT HAS GONE WRONG IN AMERICA?

I drive through my small town in Xenia, Ohio, and all I see are financial institutions and pharmacies on every corner of the town. One corner is where the bowling alley used to be. I try to find a gym where my son and his friends can practice basketball during the week and there are no facilities available for the kids, even for a fee. I drive through the city of Moraine where the General Motors plant used to be and it looks like a ghost town. And, oh yes, we now have a super Walmart that has caused many smaller stores to close.

It was November 7, 2012, the day after the Presidential election. Half the country was apparently happy and half the country remained distraught, or at least that is how it appeared based on the electoral voting results. Regardless, change in the direction of our country looks remote, especially with little shake up in Congressional incumbents and the ongoing gridlock. The only hope is to change American politics in the direction of nonpartisan cooperation with national purpose, that which is best for our country as a whole.

The destruction in the northeast from hurricane Sandy weighed heavy on our minds as another storm headed their way. Nine days later many were still without power in the face of a nor'easter that headed their way. It seems we haven't learned much from Katrina in our natural disaster cleanup efforts except that the only change happening is climate change. It also seems we have not learned from the killing sprees in our schools and public places. The recent killing spree at the Sandy Hook Elementary School in Newtown, Connecticut, by a lone gunman with mental issues has not improved our ability to identify and help persons capable of such terror. We couldn't anticipate the Boston bomber even when the U.S. was warned of the terrorist by another country, i.e., Russia.

The millions of people currently unemployed and the realities of long-term unemployment have direct effects on families' personal, economic, and emotional well-being. The federal deficit for 2012 was nearly seven times the level it was in 2007. Government debt in 2012 stood at 73 percent of GDP, twice the historical average. On the edge of the "fiscal cliff", Congress and the President could not agree on spending cuts and tax increases and so across-the-board reductions of $85 billion in federal spending, known as "sequestration", took effect March 1, 2013, along with other tax increases that had taken effect in January. These across-the-board reductions total $1.2 trillion over nine years, $85 billion of which would occur in the remaining seven months of fiscal year 13. Austerity economics is not what the economy needs at this time when it is trying to recover from one of the worst recessions since the Great Depression. We should replace the term sequestration with a "state of mind" that Congress, the President, and government officials need to acquire as a mode of operando to overspending when making budget and spending decisions.

Meanwhile, politicians argue and point fingers instead of making decisions on the size and role of the federal government and where wasteful spending can be curtailed. At the same time, corporations have not suffered. During the "recovery", corporate profits, including some non-profit organizations such as major hospitals that are exempt from taxation, soared, but companies haven't boosted hiring.

The Dow now being up "disconnect" with existing low income levels, job instability, loss of home values, and the poor mainstream economy is obviously not an indicator that the economy is recovered. Neither jobs nor wages have regained their pre-crisis highs. Home prices were still nearly 26 percent below their level when the Dow last peaked in Mar 2013, but about 14 million homeowners were underwater on their mortgages. The job market has recovered slowly, making this the worst labor market recovery since World War II.

The stock market has basically recovered back to where it was in 2000, while corporate earnings have doubled since then. I do not believe the stock market recovery is a true indication of "recovery" when Americans are still doing so poorly. Federal policies have encouraged investors into the stock market because bond yields are so low. Corporations are doing well with fewer employees and investing, instead, in technology to enhance productivity and receive tax credits and deductions.

Supply and demand for jobs keep wages low. Profits and stocks are rising but hourly wages are stagnant. Instead of these austerity measures, the government would better serve the country by providing incentives for business to expand the economy in this country, not oversees, by repairing the crumbling infrastructure, creating training and educational opportunities to correct the skills imbalance, providing research and development grants, and create other job opportunities to improve efficiencies and help the nation's people who have had their lives turned upside down through joblessness, homelessness, and natural disaster.

The **government operates on tax revenues**. Jobs create tax revenues and consequently support government services and needed social insurance programs. If there are no jobs, or wages are stagnant, people do not spend money on consumption and companies will not expand because they will have a hard time recouping their investment. So much for trickle-down economics. So the government needs to fund economic growth through public works, research and development, and other employment opportunities in collaboration with corporations and other investment opportunities. Tax reform is necessary to ensure individuals are contributing their fair share based on income and the corporate tax rate of 35 percent needs to be lowered more in line with other countries. No one can agree if we should raise taxes or lower taxes or whether our country's debt is slowing economic growth or if we should put the brakes on austerity until the recession is behind us.

We collect about $2 trillion a year in taxes but the government is spending almost $3.5 trillion. This means that $4 out of every $10 the government spends comes from borrowed money. Government's sporadic and out-of-focus spending that doesn't support national interest needs to stop. However, under spending on focused national interests can have negative impacts, including economic recovery.

Fiscal expansion is a logical response to a weak economy. If there is a demand for goods and services because employment is high then business thrives and unemployment is corrected. Creating jobs adds to tax revenue and lowers government spending on social programs. This is not to say that austerity isn't important. Government borrowing, especially on the wrong priorities, deprives the country of a chance to make a better future.

One has to ask how our country got into such a mess. Obviously, the housing crisis was the straw that broke the camel's back for our current economic woes but we didn't get into this overnight. In fact, it was a weak banking system and vast disparities in income levels that signaled the Great Depression. It has taken us decades to get into this mess again. Investment banks have taken excessive risk and "big business" (the pharmaceutical industry, oil companies, big insurance, military contractors, rich individuals, and super PACs) has been able to buy government policies through lobbyists and election funding. Long term personnel are fired, pensions are no longer funded, and investment fraud have taken life savings from many Americans.

Hedrick Smith, author of **Who Stole the American Dream?**, provides his view of how Americans have been robbed of the American dream. He explains how the American dream has been lost over the past forty years by legislative and corporate decisions that have had a direct effect on the middle class.

The cause he states began in 1971 with the "Powell Memorandum", written by Lewis Powell, a corporate lawyer who was later appointed to the Supreme Court. His memo, according to Mr. Smith, "sparked a business and corporate rebellion that would forever change the landscape of power in Washington and would influence policies and economy even now." The memo initiated transformations both in government policies and the behavior of American business leaders—causing changes to the politics and policy of the postwar era and the philosophy of giving back into the business and the economy that had provided for the prosperity of America's middle class from the mid-1940s to the mid-1970s.

According to many, wealth of the super-rich, the top one percent, rose much from 2002 to 2007 prior to the Great Recession. Lower tax rates and corporate and other tax loopholes, policy on deregulation, foreign trade, and outsourcing of jobs were all contributors to less federal government income, trade deficits, and unemployment/underemployment. Lobbyists and Super PACs continue to grow and corporations have not "trickled down" their profits, creating a break between the business and labor relationship, resulting in loss in income and pensions, and reduced job security, and less opportunity for the middle and lower classes in America.

So many agree that the current American predicament goes back to the 1970s. Wages of workers stopped keeping pace with their productivity. The profits of the top one percent continue to rise since 2007. Trickle-down economics is no longer a player. Lowering the corporate tax rate might bring some of the jobs and profits back into the economy. Many would like to see us returning tax rates on income, including dividends and interest and capital gains, to 1980 levels and eliminating some of the tax loopholes would go a long way to reduce the deficit.

Of course, reducing spending, from earmarks for pork barrel projects, procuring military systems that are not necessary, to funding federal agencies that use the funds for other than mission essential purposes (i.e. excessive executive bonuses and more), and incurring debt from mismanaged programs such as Obama care, the VA, and the lack of government enforcement of immigration policy. Oh, and let's not forget the government bailouts that some say saved our auto industry and our economy. The jury is still out on whether a lesson was learned. We should not ever have to be put in that position again.

Closing down the government in the government shutdown last fiscal year indicates the degree of political disorder in Congress. The inability of legislators to deal with legislation in an appropriate and responsible way. Holding Americans hostage to the implications of legislation or the lack of it in this case. Earmarks in legislation create havoc on our budget and our national priorities. Congress supposedly stopped the practice in 2011, but even the Continuing Resolution that reopened the government last year was loaded with earmarks.

The cumulative effect of all the problems on Americans today is why enough is enough. Stagnate wages for the middle and lower classes, outsourcing jobs overseas, risky and, in many cases, fraudulent mortgage loans, government deficit and fraud, understated inflation, lost and risky 401(k)s, loss of home values, including loss in home equity borrowed in order to stay afloat, governmental waste, inability to reduce health care and educational costs, inability to establish national and global priorities and fund appropriately, inability to contain DOD and other cost overruns in government contracts, duplication of effort among federal government agencies, excessive costs and spending on programs due to political self-interest, indecision, and gridlock. Programs such as Obamacare and all the costs associated are impacting employers, individuals, and the government, and immigration reform that has turned into a inhumane and costly crisis with the influx of children across U.S. borders and criminals, and who knows what else (terrorists), is entering our country. These problems all contribute to an increase in crime and unemployment, especially in our inner cities. And let's not forget our veterans that have made it possible that I can write and we live in freedom. There is much to do to correct their health situation, let them go to facilities that can immediately help them.

There are fundamental flaws in our political system and the policies, cost, and function of the federal government that seriously need to be corrected for this country to be the great country it once was for all those seeking the American Dream. The American dream is different and personal for each individual but the concept revolves around the ability for all people to be free to self-actualize their talents, abilities, and desires, not just for fame and fortune, but in order to live a happy and prosperous life. Thus, the American dream is about ensuring that we look out for the greater good in our policies and legislation that support opportunities for health, education, housing, research and development, innovation, jobs, and retirement. We have contracted with our government officials to carry this out. If they are not willing to act then we must react by seeking out good candidates and voting for them.

This book is an attempt to provide some common sense approaches to correcting some of the country's largest economic and political problems. I don't intend that everyone will agree with all that is written here, it is simply an effort to put out ideas and concerns that many Americans are wrestling with, but too busy to think about as they struggle with everyday life. It is just a view from a common government servant for 36 years and an American worried about our country's future and our children's and grandchildren's futures.

CHAPTER ONE
THE DOMESTIC PLAN

So here is where I suggest we need to start, assuming we have enough **elected** officials in Congress and a Presidency that will establish national and global priorities and work with corporate leaders and other government leaders to form coalitions that promote economic growth in the United States and climate change and security in the world.

I believe the Government has a role in the prosperity and equality of our society. It has a responsibility, through leadership and consciousness of our politicians and business leaders, to create laws, policy, and programs that provide for a democracy, the enforcement of laws, the creation of opportunities to sustain economic growth, and assurance that public funds are expended in a responsible manner.

In his State of the Union address, Franklin Delano Roosevelt, proclaimed that there are basic expectations by our people that make up the foundation of a healthy and strong democracy. The basic things expected involved the health of our political and economic systems. He stated they are:

"Equality of opportunity for youth and for others, jobs for those who can work, security for those who need it, the defending of those who need it, the preservation of civil liberties for all, the enjoyment of the fruits of scientific progress in a wider and constantly rising standard of living."

He warned that these basic expectations of our economic and political systems could get lost in the modern world and that the degree to which these expectations are fulfilled would be the measure of strength in these systems.

Democracy cannot be sustained if all the opportunity is contained with the one percent. I am no economist, all I can add to this discussion is common sense. What I have been able to figure out is that the economy is cyclical in nature, obviously evolving around supply and demand. Business needs demand to expand. Business expansion creates jobs. Workers need jobs to have income in order to consume and pay taxes. The government needs taxes to provide services and other economic incentives. Business is in the business to make profits. The question is just how much profit at the expense of its employees' security and product quality?

The problem is that businesses are not producing in the U.S. If they do not produce in the U.S., Americans are not working and paying taxes and businesses are not paying taxes in the U.S. Without tax revenue, the government cannot provide incentives to business without borrowing money from foreign countries, thus selling America to outsiders. The bottom line is that we need business to thrive in the U.S. and business needs to pay it forward or the whole game in America is over.

If big business, global, multinational companies like Walmart, GM, IBM, and Apple, and the "Billionaires Club", don't want to play in the U.S. then we should focus on small business in this country. There are approximately 442 billionaires in the U.S. Some 210 multi-millionaires joined the extreme wealth league last year, achieving 10-figure fortunes and the world now plays host to a record 1,426 billionaires, according to a 2014 Forbes Magazine's study. However, I would like to see these companies and the wealthy join in on a domestic plan to turn America's prosperity and opportunity around for the middle and lower classes.

The creation of a domestic plan, a bipartisan initiative including industry and government officials, needs to be the guiding light, a focus for the future. There are many initiatives the President and Congress have on their tables but, just like how the government is too big, so are the issues facing the nation. Focus on national issues is necessary now, and should be a common goal for America. The State of the Union Address was January 20, 2015. The state of the union address is designed to lay out legislative goals for Congress for the next year. However, I fear this address served politics rather than significant bipartisan opportunities for the coming year.

I propose a Domestic Plan that must be comprehensive, bipartisan, and could include the following:

Government Policy and Corporate Strategy (Public-Private Partnerships)

The smartest of the smartest need to get together and come up with a plan that finds common ground to work from with regard to taxes and other incentives for producing in the U.S. A new manifesto between the government and the small and large business enterprises in the U.S. on how best to support industry with loan guarantees, tax credits, financing plants and facilities, lowering corporate taxes, and enforcing trade agreements and/or raising tariffs on imports.

Small business and manufacturing and other businesses producing in the U.S. need government incentives to operate in the U.S. Lower corporate taxes, especially for those who operate entirely in the U.S., should be in line with other countries which are lower. Regulations that impede business growth need to be identified and analyzed for necessity.

Correcting the skills imbalance in the U.S. through apprenticeships with business would have to be established to train/retrain U.S. employees. I do not support importing skills unless it is in a field needed to fill a critical skill void or special expertise. We have a population in this country that won't be able to attend college or who are talented in fields that are not conducive to a college degree.

Experience has shown that we need to improve the industrial base and reduce the trade deficit in the U.S. in order to improve our economy and remain competitive in the world in technology and innovation. The ripple effect is improving the local economy and tax base and providing jobs to millions. Creative partnerships with government and business will be necessary, along with grants, subsidies and other incentives.

Tax Code Reform

The majority of Americans want the tax code simplified, including the IRS. It would make the IRS's job a lot easier with regard to interpretation of tax loop holes, exemptions, deductions and exclusions that may give the IRS too much power. One way to simplify the tax code is to make it fair for all based on income but what is considered income? The corporate tax rate needs to be lower to enable business to be competitive and to avoid corporate inversions. Tax recommendations should include lower corporate tax rates from the 35 percent top rate (the highest in the industrialized world) to 20 percent or so. We need to put U.S. corporations in a competitive position with other countries that have lower corporation taxes. The U.S. tax law encourages companies to move to other countries with lower corporate tax rates and keep their profits abroad because they're taxed only if they are repatriated to the U.S. Many U.S. companies are moving their companies overseas, much due to corporate tax rates, cheap labor and other incentives; nearly 50 have done so since 2005 and more expected.

Some suggest an increase in capital gains tax to the level income is taxed, many say possibly adding a super tax imposed for millionaires, lower taxes for incomes less than $138,925, add more tax brackets above the current top bracket of $388,350 and increase the rate. Others recommend eliminating the Bush tax reductions for taxpayers making over $250,000 a year and the tax exemption for profits made overseas, and tax breaks and loopholes for the very rich, and remove the $106,800 cap on payroll tax. Those would require debate and further consideration with entire tax reform that probably will not happen anytime soon.

Energy Independence and Innovation

We need an "Energy Plan." The energy balance is necessary at this time due to the fragile economy, the current and future gas and oil costs, and our dependency and other country's reliance on foreign oil. It is not that pollution should be avoided but in this fragile economy in the U.S. we cannot avoid pollution at all costs, just like we cannot implement austerity programs when we are trying to bring our economy back, not that austerity isn't a needed program, but it needs to be institutionalized in a long term approach to avoid overspending, project by project, that is not needed for the national interest.

Coal industry currently provides 40 percent of the energy usage. EPA and executive order policy may be hurting business and increasing costs to consumers, neither of which we need at this time. Oil and gas regulations increase costs as well and need to be looked at now.

We need to focus on the development of the oil pipeline, natural gas, and clean energy technologies. The Keystone XL Pipeline Project has the potential to reduce the amount of oil America imports but the jury is still out on where the oil will actually be exported to and maybe it only reduces costs for Canada. We do know it will provide jobs, an economic boost to the U.S. It may also reduce environmental hazards from trucking and wear and tear of our highways. Fracking has been controversial as well, especially from environmental groups. Apparently the Department of Energy now says it is safe to our water system. Fracking would create jobs, increase the tax base, lower energy costs, and is considered as a safer than some other alternatives.

Government grants to foster innovation and solutions to meet our energy needs would create jobs and encourage young adults to work in this area with internships and other focused programs. Again, we need collaboration with our government, industry and students and other talented individuals.

Immigration

America loves immigrants, we are all immigrates in our heritage. We are also a country of laws and a country that that spends a lot of money on our needy people but we have to balance what we do for non-Americans with what we do for our own people. We give vast amounts of money to other countries, Africa most recently. But Americans are weary, when do we balance our giving with our most sacred possession, our children and families in America. This immigration issue is forcing the conversation. Invasion of illegal immigrants over the past several years, including 60,000 children recently and more expected monthly, crossing our southern borders through Mexico from Central America, needs to be contained as it is inhumane, costly, and not fair to our citizens and those who are in line and following the law to gain U.S. citizenship. It is estimated the recent border crossings will total 34,000 people per month. Our number one priority with this issue should be to adequately secure our borders and stop the financial disaster and health concerns associated with allowing them into our country illegally.

We need to change the 2008 Wilberforce law, finish building a fence on the border, and use other technology to control the border such as drones, cameras, and ground sensors. We cannot afford to take care of these immigrants, especially when our jobs have gone overseas, and we need to control the crime and health issues that also comes into the country with this problem. Then, after we are able to control our borders, do what is right for the immigrants, their families, and the security of our country. We need to know who the 11 million undocumented immigrants are for security reasons. Providing amnesty to five million is a dangerous precedent and unfair to those currently in line for citizenship. The Border States and the U.S. have spent millions and billions, respectively, on the border security but it hasn't solved the problem. We haven't had the border under control for many years, many administrations. The law needs to be enforced, money won't help if the law is not followed. Sequestration has and will limit the number of border control officers. Illegal is illegal in this country. That is what we always thought. For those needing refuge should be made aware of the process to expedite application in the countries they live in instead of making the dangerous trip to the border.

Infrastructure Development

According to the American Society of Civil Engineers (ASCE), the U.S. gets a "D" grade in the condition of our nation's bridges, highways, dams, railways, waterways, ports, water systems, and tunnels. According to the World Economic Forum, the ranking of our infrastructure has dropped from first to sixteenth since 2006.

Government start-up funds to attract private investment in financing U.S. infrastructure is what is needed. Hiring of high school graduates can be an added benefit and training program to enable inner city youth to have opportunities that are fruitful to themselves and their families. A leg up and the opportunity to gain skills and a positive attitude toward life.

Research and Education

In science, high tech research and development, Science, Technology, Engineering and Mathematics (STEM), innovation, and inventions, we are falling behind other countries. We have many illnesses that are crippling to people that could benefit from scientific research, as they struggle daily. This is exciting. There are so many areas we could see to fruition if we allowed our talented to pursue their dreams. Again it is priorities.

Consolidate agencies involved in these efforts and provide government and private financing of our most crucial needs. Send highly qualified students from our country identified by the schools to college to learn and develop prototypes we can implement. This provides an incentive to work in exchange for a college education, with a job to follow.

This country cannot even provide pencils and paper to some of our school children. This is the foundation of our educational system. This is where we need to start. This is ridiculous to think we have so little to contribute to our children and their education. Then there is the issue of a lack of food and nutrition for our children. Then we need to modernize the educational system and make it available to more at a lower cost. On-line education should be less expensive and accessible to more. Students can study and learn at their own pace. Cost control with regard to higher education needs to be addressed at least at the state level.

Climate Change and War

Climate change is a global problem, just as are the many military conflicts we find our country involved in for humanitarian and security reasons with our military. You ask how these are the same. They both involve the expenditure of money and lives the U.S. does not have to carry out for the benefit of the world. The U.S. cannot save the world on these fronts because the threats and dangers effect all countries in the world we share. We need a global effort to ignite the United Nations and NATO to contain those who threaten our democracy and our environment. These efforts cannot be accomplished without a global coalition and the U.S. needs to show clear leadership in foreign policy with our allies. The terrorist threat is far more immediate, as is the Ebola scare. Countries with the most pollution, i.e. China, need to be dealt with in some comprehensive manner.

All nations need to share the concern over terrorism as it is still growing currently with Hamas, ISIS and others. The threat of nuclear proliferation is also always on the horizon. We need a foreign policy strategy to prevent crisis instead of reacting to a crisis. We need U.S. diplomacy on a constant basis, not just at times of crisis. Intelligence was never more important. We need to use technology and a modernized military to secure our readiness and national security. Boots on the ground should be used if the Department of Defense so recommends. They are the experts. The country is war weary and we have lost so many lives and gone further into debt but the mission of freedom must be upheld.

What is the "red line" for Americans when it comes to U.S. involvement in foreign countries? Whatever it is it needs to be consistent and agreements with countries need to be lived up to. Here are some ideas:

Threat to the U.S. national security, direct or indirect? Humanitarian causes, genocide, other types of mass murder? Terrorism, ISIS and Hamas for example, are a threat that needs to be extinguished, whatever it takes. We have military for national security, even if we are war weary, we have to stand up to those who mean destruction against the U.S. and a strategy, preferably with our ally nations, to contain this threat on a long term basis.

CHAPTER TWO
FEDERAL GOVERNMENT REFORM

"We the People of the United States, in Order to form a more perfect Union, establish Justice, insure domestic Tranquility, provide for the common defense, promote the general Welfare, and secure the Blessings of Liberty to ourselves and our Posterity, do ordain and establish this Constitution for the United States of America."

The above is the preamble to the U.S. Constitution. The constitution is the backbone of our democracy as envisioned by our forefathers. We can't discuss federal government reform without first looking at the role of the President and the executive branch of government.

The United States Presidency

Article II of the U.S. Constitution states that the executive power shall be vested in a President of the United States of America. The primary power of the executive branch rests with the president, who chooses his vice president, and his Cabinet members who head the federal departments of the executive branch of government. The executive is the part of government that has sole authority and responsibility for the daily administration of the federal government. The President, with the Vice President and Cabinet members, are responsible for carrying out the functions of the executive branch of our government. The executive branch executes or enforces the law, serves as head of state, and is the Commander-in-Chief of the armed forces.

So you cannot discuss federal government reform without discussing the scandals and fraud occurring within many of our federal government agencies and the responsibility of the President and his Cabinet. The President is responsible for running the federal government and for leadership in foreign policy.

Federal government agencies have grown in size much due to what I call "Institutional Building". Many federal agencies have lost any accountability for their mismanagement. Metrics have been driving the wrong behavior outcomes and abuse of widespread senior executive bonuses and extreme mismanagement abound. The Veteran Administration is a prime example of this. However, VA, IRS, and the DOD agencies, in particular, have also had their missions expanded over the years with the Iraq and Afghanistan wars, vast increase in the number of veterans, and increased responsibly placed under the IRS due to new federal policy, including Obamacare. Therefore, mission is the critical element in determining workforce needs. Policies and "projects" organizations come up with, sometimes just to have their name on something, can also create "make work" that can add to workload and inefficiency in implementing the mission in an organization.

Obamacare was not well thought out and is now costing unrealistic amounts of money for the government, businesses, and its citizens. In this case, politicians and the President didn't even read the legislation prior to enactment. Citizens are falling through the cracks, the very ones the legislation was trying to help. Their income is too high to qualify for Medicare but they do not have the income sufficient to afford Obamacare. And, if states did not agree to expand Medicare, poor individuals have nothing to assist them. We should have targeted those who needed healthcare and not those that did not need it. Now companies have been driven to cancel spousal health care, reduce employee hours to part time, etc., to avoid the law.

The border crisis has been escalating for years because the government, many presidents, haven't enforced current law and processes established for immigration and left the border unsecure. Thanks to Congress, funding the border control was reduced last year and for 10 years to come due to the across the board budget cuts known as sequestration. The President has released illegal immigrants from jail, 65,000 or more of them recently, and did not deport them. Many of those that are deported return to the U.S. repeatedly, two recently killing a border control agent. Since the 2008 law allowing certain unaccompanied minors the right to a hearing and, more recently, the 2012 executive order that stopped the deportation of young illegal immigrants who entered the United States as children if they meet certain requirements, thousands have been entering and are not being deported. The unsecure border has been a problem for years without successful initiatives to adequately secure the border. This is a no brainer. Common sense tells you that securing the border is the first priority in addressing the immigrant invasion and no legislation is necessary to do this. Enforcing the U.S. law on the process to use to become a legal immigrant is also necessary. Now this is costing millions of tax dollars unnecessarily.

Foreign policy and America's leadership in the world appears to have fallen short. Red lines are drawn but no action is taken to back them up. Turmoil in Iran and Iraq, Russia in the Ukraine, Syria, Central America, Egypt, Africa, and Israel has been evolving for a long time now. The Administration has not been proactive or successful in developing a world strategy with our allies to fight the expansion of terrorism and mass killing of innocent people across the world.

I began this book the day after the 2012 presidential election. The election was supposedly won due to the Latino, black, and youth vote. Ironically, we now have crisis on the border with illegal immigrants and minors spilling into our country and threatening our health and safety, jobs, the budget, and opportunities to Americans in the U.S., especially in the inner cities where they will compete for jobs, schools, health care, and other dwindling resources. Obama ran his 2008 and 2012 campaigns on hope and change. Politics were not supposed to interfere with doing the right thing. No more politics as usual. Jobs would be created for the young adults, but many are currently living back home with their parents. So the young adults voted for Obama and they are still living at home.

So what does the next president look like? What are the essential credentials necessary to govern this great nation? Here are some ideas: 1) Vision of the direction the country needs to head; 2) Past accomplishments, experience in governance, and perhaps experience in business; 3) Leadership in making decisions and in uniting people toward a common cause with action even if the result is uncertain. These may be some credentials to look at when choosing a president. These are nonpartisan credentials. Nowhere did we say they had to have the ability to raise campaign funding, did we? Washington, Lincoln, Jefferson, and Roosevelt come to mind for most of Americans.

The current President claimed he heard of some of these government agency scandals first from watching the TV news. This is not proactive management of the federal government. Who is minding the store? The

American people are caring less and less about political parties as they feel the party system is actually the cause of legislative gridlock and policies that support private interest groups and campaign and reelection instead of doing what is right for the country.

President George Washington, in his farewell address to the nation, September 19, 1796, urged Americans to avoid excessive political party spirit and geographical distinctions. He warned Americans of the political dangers they must avoid if they are to remain true to their values. So, for the sake of unity, we should not allow political party caucuses to overtake the values of America for the sake of a political party. In an excerpt from the address he talks about unity by common cause and the work of joint efforts as follows:

"Citizens by birth or choice of a common country, that country has a right to concentrate your affections. The name of AMERICAN, which belongs to you, in your national capacity, must always exalt the just pride of Patriotism, more than any appellation derived from local discriminations. With slight shades of difference, you have the same Religion, Manners, Habits, and Political Principles. You have in a common cause fought and triumphed together; the Independence and Liberty you possess are the work of joint counsels, and joint efforts—of common dangers, sufferings, and successes."

When Mitt Romney was running for President in 2012 many of us hoped that if he was elected he would run the federal government like a successful business. I think he focused on fund raising and campaigning and he may have forgotten why he really wanted to run for president. So much for focusing on campaign financing and not on the people he was really trying to help. So, can the government be run like a business? Businesses are in the business of making money, period. That being said, what is important is how they go about making profits. Do their employees have pensions, healthcare, and decent pay?

The government is or should be in the business of carrying out necessary programs and functions to serve a public mission. Unless the entity is self- sustaining, most government entities are providing a service for free and not trying to make a profit. Service based rather than profit based.

Incompetent employees are not easy to fire. Disciplinary problems and nonperformance have to be documented and supervisors are reluctant to do what is necessary to start the formal removal process for unsatisfactory performance. Incentives for saving money or creating innovations and processes that produce cost savings and efficiencies should be rewarded verses the current "spending" practices we will discuss later in this chapter. Executives and leadership need to embrace these types of values all the way to the President instead of allowing these executives to remain unaccountable for not managing their "business" in an effective and efficient manner.

Agencies need to be held to metrics and performance results that drive desired results and are continually monitored to ensure the mission of the agency is still on target and has not out grown its mission and function. Perhaps instead of profit, as in the private sector, the government should be held to manage its "business" in an efficient and effective manner toward a desired outcome, like patient care in the case of the VA. The larger the government becomes, the less transparent it is unless leadership is held accountable at the highest levels. It is the nature of the beast that, unless controlled based on certain measures, the government is self-perpetuated, hiring and promoting who they want and, first and foremost, securing their stature in the organization. Measuring performance and looking for improved processes, meeting or improving on contractual overruns, utilizing value based contracts, delivering products on time are all measureable.

The Proliferation of the Federal Government

The federal government has grown to mass proportions since the Depression through the 1970s (especially 1960), much due to increased domestic responsibilities, including social programs like, social security, Medicare, and welfare, food stamps, housing, etc. However, many more agencies and oversight departments continued to arise, some due to the states' inability to govern as democratic institutions since the Great Depression and through the end of WW II up to the 1960s. Reversing some of the "institutional building" over the past decades needs to occur. **It is crucial that we identify the true role of the federal government and ensure critical missions are not impacted by lack of funding.** This would ultimately entail reductions in military, civilians, and the contractor workforce. Therefore, careful study is required to reorganize and consolidate functions and realign the current workforce, slowing down on new hiring except where skills imbalances exist. Employees who do not adequately perform need to be fired but the Office of Personnel Management (OPM) rules require much performance documentation to remove an employee. Programs that should not be managed by the federal government or that duplicate effort among other agencies or the private sector need to be identified and eliminated on a regular basis.

The three branches of government cost the federal government $185 billion in payroll and the government has a $17 trillion national debt. The amount of interest expense was $359.8 billion in the fiscal year ending September 2012. According to a Governmental Accounting Office (GAO) report, the major cost areas within the federal government operations are payments, oversight/compliance, property management, redundancy, contract resource management, technology, workforce, and acquisitions/procurement.

Entitlement programs already account for nearly 62 percent of all federal spending. However, a lot of fraud exists with the Medicare system, social security disability, and the welfare programs. Surplus funds from social security have been used to "borrow from Peter to pay Paul." When we have had surpluses in our entitlement programs, the federal government has used the surpluses to fund other priorities. This type of barrowing seems risky and the government should be forced to find other means or reprioritize, period.

The federal government has proliferated into programs and departments that actually duplicate purpose and expenditures or that are not appropriate for funding and management by the federal government. This is the analysis that needs to be undertaken and every department, program, and expenditure should undergo a "test" to prove effectiveness and efficiency, purpose for existence, mission, federal appropriateness, and duplication of effort. Creation of a federal agencies and sunset provisions for continuing the life of an agency should be imposed and metrics established to measure results. Institution building is costly.

We have to do what is right for our country when it comes to decisions on how our government revenue is spent. Decisions cannot be made based on personal or political desires. We owe it the future of the country and our children who will inherit the effects of this type of government operation to make spending decisions with consciousness, but not by using sequestration's mindless across-the-board budget cut strategy. Budgets represent choices and priorities. Government officials, Congress, and the President need to take leadership control over spending with establishing criteria that must be met to justify spending. Where are our priorities? You have to look at the mission of agencies, no across the board cuts, please.

- Is this a national priority?

- Is this a role of the federal government as outlined in the U.S. Constitution?

- Does it support a Domestic Plan?

- Is it essential for our national security?

The government needs to reward savings and efficiencies by its personnel and the use of incentive vehicles in government contracts. It must disband the federal budget practice of rewarding organizations that spend all the monies allotted in a fiscal year by allotting the same or more the next year. There is no incentive to be cost effective and efficient. The federal government needs to allow the unspent monies to be returned to the government at the end of the fiscal year or allow agencies to carryover the funds into the next fiscal year. There is a rule within governmental agencies that monies allocated must be spent or less monies will be allocated in the next fiscal year. This is a mindset and a practice that needs to be changed and we need to create an environment that rewards effectiveness and efficiency.

However, on the contrary, the federal government cannot be set up to fail either. Military need to be available and trained to provide support where needed, even the Benghazi attack might have been caught up in the sequestration when additional support was not provided. Agencies must be staffed to perform their functions. For example, Congress keeps giving the Internal Revenue Service more and more complex assignments while giving it less and less money. The agency's budget has declined every year since 2010. Congress has required it to address everything from health-care reform to campaign finance to the Foreign Account Tax Compliance Act (FATCA). FATCA aims to build on recent successful crackdowns on Americans hiding their money overseas. At the same time, the Internal Revenue Service (IRS) workforce decreased by 9 percent from 2010 to the end of 2012, according to a 2013 Treasury Inspector General for Tax Administration Report.

Change the Roles of the Federal Government

Sorting out functions of government (federal government verses state and local governments), or as Alice M. Rivlin, author of *"Reviving the American Dream, The Economy, the States, and the Federal Government,"* calls it "Dividing the job" involves devolution of whole federal functions to the states."

The federal government has expanded since the depression primarily due to increased social programs. The roles of the federal government should be reduced and limited to those authorized by the U. S. Constitution. I normally do not think establishing commissions to study and report back to Congress is an effective way to make change because rarely are the reports utilized. However, in this case, it would require a single body to sort out the appropriate missions and agency roles and eliminate duplication of effort among agencies.

This type of reform would require the establishment of a commission made up of the Governmental Accounting Office (GAO), the Office of Management and Budget (OMB), state governors, cabinet heads, subject matter experts to not only study the issue and provide specific recommendations but also create a process to oversee and to establish clear missions and performance metrics for the remaining agencies. The following is my recommended baseline for "dividing the job" of the federal government. The federal government should have responsibility for:

- Regulation, inspection, oversight (health & safety, environment, economy, health care cost control, grants & loans)

- National Security

- Taxation

- Social Insurance Programs

- International issues

- Law enforcement

- Intelligence

The federal government could provide grants and subsidies to the states or private investment to support the following missions:

- Research & development

- Education and Skills Training

- Highways

- Natural disasters

- Housing, welfare, food stamps, Medicaid, child care

- Economic Development

Oversight—Follow the Money— Eliminate Fraud, Waste, and Abuse

Fraud, waste, and abuse cost the federal government billions of dollars annually in improper payments. For example, in Fiscal Year (FY)11 the federal government reported $115 billion was Medicare fraud.

Regulatory conformance and fleshing out fraud, waste and abuse within and against the federal government should be a top priority of the federal government. This type of oversight of funds allotted should be an important function of the Inspector General (IG), OMB and the GAO.

The core mission of the OMB is to serve the President of the United States in implementing his vision across the Executive Branch. OMB is the largest component of the Executive Office of the President. It reports directly to the President and helps a wide range of executive departments and agencies across the Federal Government to implement the commitments and priorities of the President. This office should be the implementation and enforcement arm of the executive branch of the government and oversee the efficiencies and effectiveness of federal agencies.

The GAO was established as the General Accounting Office by the Budget and Accounting Act of 1921. The act requires the GAO to investigate all matters relating to the receipt, disbursement, and application of public funds and report to the President and Congress on recommendations for greater economy or efficiency in public expenditures. According to the GAO's current mission statement, the agency exists to support the Congress in meeting its constitutional responsibilities and to help improve the performance and ensure the accountability of the federal government for the benefit of the American people. The Government Accountability Office is an independent agency which provides to the United States Congress audit, evaluation, and investigative services. As such, it is part of the legislative branch of the United States government.

In the annual GAO reports on duplication and cost savings you will find areas of fragmentation, overlap, and duplication, as well as opportunities for cost savings and revenue enhancement for the federal government. This body of work is in response to the statutory requirement that GAO identify and report annually on federal programs, agencies, offices and initiatives which have duplicative goals or activities.

In addition to identifying new areas, the GAO monitors the progress executive branch agencies and Congress have made in addressing the areas previously identified. There is a publicly accessible on-line search tool that tracks and provides the implementation status of every suggested action that the GAO has identified in its three annual reports. For example, to date, 65 actions have been addressed, 149 actions have been partially addressed, and 85 actions have not been addressed.

If the federal government does not implement the recommendations, this is, in its self, inefficiency and ineffectiveness. The whole issue of "before you cut spending find the savings" applies here.

The GAO should work with the OMB and federal agencies to ensure there are procedures in place to prevent fraud, waste, and abuse. Federal grants and aide that are misused need to be returned to the federal government and prosecution should be initiated if necessary. For example, the Department of Energy invested in an electric car company named Fisker Automotive. Fisker laid off a majority of its workers after receiving $192 million in federal aid as part of the Obama administration's Advanced Technology Vehicles Manufacturing loan program, designed to aid car companies pursuing energy efficiency. And then there was the Solyndra case were tax payers and private investors lost millions.

In the case of DELFI, the government actually allowed bailout to union workers whose pensions were saved but the other nonunion workers lost their pensions. A recent GAO audit discovered that three United States Department of Agriculture agencies had made $36 million in improper payments to 6,336 dead people between 2008 and 2012. The USDA spends $20 billion annually on programs that support one million participants through income assistance, crop insurance and disaster relief. According to GAO official Daniel Garcia-Diaz on a GAO's Watchdog Report podcast, "Over the course of time, farmers who are enrolled in these programs may pass away. If nobody notifies USDA or the agency doesn't have any particular steps to identify deceased farmers, it's possible that payments or other benefits may accrue to deceased individuals." There are many more examples in the GAO reports and elsewhere.

The U.S. Department of Agriculture, already known for paying benefits to deceased farmers, incorrectly overpaid $20.3 million in financial assistance during 2012, reports the USDA inspector general.

Excessive performance awards were given to Veteran Affairs personnel in the form of bonuses where actual non-performance was documented. During fiscal year 2011, about 18,000 of the 22,500 doctors and dentists employed by the Veterans Health Administration were awarded performance bonus, at a cost to taxpayers of about $150 million. It may be found that these bonuses were used as incentives to keep doctors and other professionals on the VA payroll. Exurbanite bonuses were also paid to 80 percent of the Senior Executive Service (SES) within the VA creating a culture of abuse.

Almost 200 major Information technology (IT) investments were at medium to high risk of failure, according to the GAO and OMB. According to the Washington Post, at least $10 billion in federal technology contracts are currently at risk of failing, according to a new review by the Government Accountability Office — and the number could be larger.

The GAO's Information technology (IT) management director, David A. Powner, outlined the findings at a hearing of the Senate subcommittee on efficiency and effectiveness of government programs. "Information technology should enable government to better serve the American people. However, despite spending hundreds of billions on IT since 2000, the federal government has experienced failed IT projects and has achieved little of the productivity improvements that private industry has realized from IT," Powner said in written testimony.

Office of the Inspector General (OIG) is an office that is part of Cabinet departments and independent agencies of the federal government as well as some state and local governments. Each office includes an Inspector General who is charged with identifying and investigating fraud, waste, abuse, and mismanagement within its own agency.

The Permanent Subcommittee on Investigations released the findings of an 18-month investigation that found evidence used by the Social

Security Administration to award disability benefits was deficient. The investigation found that more than a quarter of 300 randomly selected case files were awarded benefits without properly addressing insufficient, contradictory and incomplete evidence.

It is critical that Congress oversea the sustainability and long-term vitality of our safety net programs. Those who are fraudulently placed on disability rolls by the Social Security Administration take money from the tax payer and leave less for those who really are deserving. With the flood of applications more have to wait to have their applications processed.

The Committee on Oversight and Government Reform is a U.S. House of Representatives committee that has existed in varying forms since 1816. The Committee's government-wide oversight jurisdiction and expanded legislative authority make it one of the most influential and powerful committees in the House.

It seems these agencies and committees should work together as their missions are similar and overlapping. If we could make this mission of identifying and criminalizing fraud, waste, and abuse we could save and prevent loss of government revenue. Once social security disability is approved, it is approved for life. Perhaps we need to relook at that policy since we are finding so much fraud in the program.

The Department of Defense (DOD) has a clear role in national security. The 10-year sequestration across-the-board reductions will be applied equally to the DOD as it is to the other federal agencies unless it is repealed by Congress. Even though across the board cuts are not the smartest way to achieve savings, it does force a new way of "rethinking" decisions that have been made in the past, in many cases through legislation that may need to be reined back in. Whether for political reasons or "institution building" purposes, the government has a lot of areas where it can look for and find opportunities to reduce, reorganize, and disband organizations and programs.

Former U.S. Senator Tom A. Coburn, M.D., (R-OK), who was the former ranking member of the Homeland Security and Governmental Affairs Committee, authored the report entitled *Department of Everything*, November 2012. In the report he shows how the DOD spending in many cases has nothing to do with national security. He states similarly to what I stated above in The Proliferation of the Federal Government section, "The threat of our national debt can be defeated by reviewing every department, every program and expenditure within the federal budget, including the DOD. We must eliminate waste and duplication to refocus the Pentagon to its true mission: fighting and winning the nation's wars."

Some examples he discusses are research projects that have little or nothing to do with national defense or medical needs related to military service. He claims that education opportunities for the military duplicate the Department of Education and local efforts and the DOD Military Tuition Assistance that provides college funding for military members and duplicates the Department of Veteran Affairs; duplicative and unnecessary alternative energy research by DOD; Pentagon-run grocery stores in the U.S.; and military members performing civilian-type job functions and too many generals.

Former U.S. Senator Tom A. Coburn, M.D. also authored the *Wastebook 2013*. Sen. Coburn highlights inappropriate use of taxpayer money in programs, grants, projects and contracts, including $200 billion every year through fraud, waste, duplication and mismanagement and low-priority spending totaling nearly $30 billion.

Some examples of wasteful spending highlighted in *Wastebook 2013* include: Uncle Sam Looking for Romance on the Web – (NEH) $914,000; Mass Destruction of Weapons – (Department of Defense) $7 billion; Millions Spent Building, Promoting an Insurance Plan Few Want and a Website that Doesn't Work – (Department of Health and Human Services) At least $379 million; Government Study Finds Out Wives Should Calm Down (NIH) $325,525; Fort Hood Shooter Continued to Collect Government Paycheck (Army) ($52,952 in 2013);

NASA Searches for Signs of Intelligent Life... in Congress – (NASA) $3 million; Hurricane Sandy "Emergency" Funds Spent on TV Ads ($65 million); Federally Funded Solar Panels Covered at Manchester-Boston Airport Because the Glare Blinds Pilots and Controllers (FAA) - $3.5 million; A grant from NSF that went to a company in North Carolina to develop a math learning game based on the zombie apocalypse; and NASA's Little Green Man (NASA) — $390,000.

Other non DOD waste included in the *Wastebook* include highlights like: the State Department spent $630,000 to attract followers to its Facebook and Twitter accounts; NASA is spending $3 million to study how Congress works; the National Endowment for the Humanities spent nearly a million dollars over three years to explore the origins of popular romance in multi-media; and taxpayers have so far spent $319 million to build the Healthcare.gov website and estimates project that more than twice that will be spent on publicity and marketing.

Eliminate Duplication of Effort Among Federal Agencies and Programs

A 2013 GAO report uncovered 162 areas of duplicate spending. Duplication of effort or the mission of federal agencies and programs would also be analyzed as part of any review of "dividing the job" as discussed earlier in this chapter. This duplication of programs within agencies occurs when Congress passes laws, similar to earmarks that were used until 2011 to spend on programs or projects within their districts. The President is responsible for the administration of the executive branch but oversight of such programs is difficult without a data base to identify duplication. Actually, the data system would be necessary at the time legislation is drafted, before it becomes law.

Having worked as a bill drafter and legislative analyst, it seems to me that a data base could identify similarities in existing programs and initiatives prior to voting on legislation. All legislation drafted at the state level in West Virginia always summarized the cost and impact of any legislation. This problem of duplication is extremely costly to taxpayers. It would be better to identify such duplication before passage than after. There are some 1,362 programs that have been identified by the U.S. Government Accountability Office.

We have all heard of the "bridge to nowhere." Seriously, there needs to be a way where legislation is reviewed before introduced on the floor to identify if the imitative is already on the books or resides under another agency.

Change the Federal Budget Process

The federal government must disband the federal budget practice of rewarding organizations that spend all the monies allotted in a fiscal year by allotting the same or more the next year. There is no incentive to be cost effective and efficient utilizing the practice. The federal government needs to allow the unspent monies to be returned to the government at the end of the fiscal year or allow it to be rolled over to next fiscal year and discontinue the current practice of spending all monies prior to the end of the fiscal year. The monies cannot be turned back in and used in the next fiscal year to reduce next year funding requirements. Instead, agencies are actually rewarded with funding for the next fiscal year if they used all the funds allotted the prior fiscal year. This practice must stop and allow for better stewardship of program dollars and eliminate year end wasteful spending.

Office of Personnel Management (OPM) Guidelines

OPM guidelines need to be changed to allow more flexibility for the grade levels that match position responsibility and skills, and no longer force the building of organizations that must support the numbers supervised and grade levels in the organization. This only contributes to government growth and overpayment of human capital resources. We can no longer afford to allow empire building in the federal government.

We must move in the other direction and reduce numbers of federal workers and allow grade levels that match the responsibilities of the position and the mission of the organization, without building an entire empire with supervisors and supporting grade levels.

The federal government establishes civilian positions under the guidelines of the OPM. These guidelines are well established and inflexible in nature. Federal Classification and Job Grading System is used to determine the pay plan, series, title, and grade for most work in the Federal Government. It includes grading criteria for the General Schedule (GS) and Federal Wage Classification System positions. The law requires the Office of Personnel Management (OPM) to define Federal occupations, establish official position titles, and describe the grades of various levels of work. To fulfill this responsibility, OPM approves and issues position classification standards that must be used by agencies to determine the title, series, and grade of positions covered by title 5.

"Position management" is an agency's process of establishing and maintaining positions in order to perform the agency's legally assigned work in the most effective and efficient manner. Organizations and agencies of the federal government are built within the federal government based on a grade structure that can lend to overstaffing and higher grade staffing just to support the organizational level and supervisory grade structure. For instance, if a Senior Executive Service (SES) member heads the organization, there will be one or more General Schedule (GS)-15s in the organization reporting to the SES and each GS-15 will have one or more GS-14s in the organization reporting to the GS-15 and on and on it goes down to the GS-4 level. In the military, there may also be a general officer heading the organization and an SES deputy and one or more GS-15s and on and on down it goes.

CHAPTER THREE
CONGRESSIONAL REFORM

Let's just say, our American government is struggling to govern. Many of our government officials are more about party politics and pointing fingers than governing. I don't see much of anything happening on the domestic front, like securing our borders, lowering corporate tax rates to keep business in the U.S., or on foreign policy that draws a "red" line with a comprehensive strategy on what America's role should be in combating terrorism in any form. Congress hasn't passed an appropriations bill in seven years. Who is governing our country? Political parties are preventing the country from governance. It has become survival of party and party leadership instead of survival of our people and our nation as we have known it. Legislators vote on party lines when they do vote on anything. Party leadership controls committee chairman selection and committee membership and selectively keeps legislation from being introduced on the floor of Congress. Former Senate Majority Leader Harry Reid is a prime example of this behavior. Now, even with the republican majority in both chambers, the President threatens to veto legislation before it is even introduced in in Congress.

Our federal intelligence agencies don't talk to each other, so what do we do, after September 11, 2001, when the World Trade Center in New York, the Pentagon in Washington D.C., and an airplane that crashed in Pennsylvania, was attacked? We create another federal agency to communicate among existing agencies, the Homeland Security Agency. It is now 13 years later and we are now fighting a worse terrorist group, ISIS or "ISIL." More reason to have a sustained effort in the world with support from all effected countries.

For several decades America has become less and less a nation where all classes share to some degree in the country's prosperity as it did for decades following World War II. Many of our political leaders have sided with the lobbyists and been consumed by reelection and campaign funding, causing public policies and economic favor to special interests and big business. Congress and the President are divided, Congress itself is divided, as well as the political parties within themselves. Spending priorities are not debated and are not ones that support national interest and general welfare.

Decisions on legislation needed for such things as tax reform, reversing the federal debt, banking and financial reform, immigration, reducing the size of the federal government to name a few are not being made. The showdown between Democrats and Republicans and Republicans within themselves could not be more exemplified than with the FY14 Budget Bill, the debt limit measure, and the funding of the Affordable Care Act. Legislation should be voted on separately and not use the practice of horse trading to undermine the passage of fundamental legislation like the Budget Bill and raising the debt limit. Lack of unity in Congress resulted in a government shutdown and the near first-ever federal default.

The challenge we face is the "consciousness" I referred to in the prologue of this book. We face losing our democracy if we can't return to the values and principles our country was founded on. Americans have lost some of these values and so has our political base. Politicians allow themselves to be bought out by lobbyists and big business in return for reelection which effects where federal funding is appropriated and where it is not appropriated. It effects the policies and laws in favor of the wealthy, big business, banking and financial institutions at the expense of investing in education, small business and manufacturing, highways and crumbling infrastructure, science, and research and development. Businesses no longer invest in economic growth, the community, or their employees' pay and retirement plans. Lifelong pensions have become 401(k)s and pay has remained stagnant. Health care subsidies are replacing company health care plans. Higher education costs are out of the ball park and need to be reined in.

How can so many produce so little? The legislative branch consists of the Senate and the House of Representatives, collectively known as Congress. There are 100 senators; each state has two. Each state has a different number of representatives, with the number determined by the state's population. At present, there are 435 members of the House. The legislative branch is charged with passing the nation's laws and allocating funds for running of the federal government and providing assistance to the states. Right now they are not capable of doing either. "We the People" are responsible for electing members of congress. That is where our power lies, along with urging our members to change its rules and procedures on how Congressional leadership is selected and how our states should open primary elections to all without regard to party affiliation as is done in several states. We can also support public campaign efforts to help know our candidates without having to rely on large campaign funding. Who we elect to congress can impact our lives; jobs, economy, incomes, homes, and retirements.

As we discussed in the previous chapter, 62 percent of the federal budget is dedicated to mandatory programs, referred to as entitlements. This spending is mandated by law and most of the funds come from payroll deductions and employer contributions. The programs include social security, Medicare, Medicaid, unemployment compensation, food stamps, and interest on our national debt. That leaves a little over a third of spending to go to discretionary programs that the President and Congress must negotiate every year, including the Department of Defense and all other federal government activities. The passage of appropriation bills is a prime role of Congress, yet it has been many years since this process has been successful. Instead of a House and Senate appropriations committee process that analyzes budget line items, the leadership has been passing piecemeal funding in continuing resolutions to keep the government running.

It was Tuesday, Oct 1st 2013, and I had just been sent home due to furlough, along with approximately 800,000 other civilian federal workers. The federal government had shut down for the first time since 1995. On Thursday, Oct 17th 2013, the Senate got credit for coming up with a bipartisan agreement to end fiscal impasse, not. The bipartisan "agreement" negotiated by former Majority Leader Harry Reid and former Minority Leader Mitch McConnell did not really include any substance or compromise, only earmarks. All it did was extend the current situation out for months and provide Senator McConnell's home state of Kentucky with $2.918 billion in funding for a dam project on the Ohio River. I understand that Congress raised discretionary spending above the bipartisan Budget Control Act of 2011 limit by $45 billion for 2014 and $18 billion for 2015.

This chapter will require creative writing and perhaps deductive reasoning that I will throw out for contemplation! It might be easier if Washington DC would make pot legal, maybe that would help break the gridlock! Some say we just need a new President but there is enough wrong with Congress and their inability to perform their job. Record low approval ratings have been recorded for both the President and Congress. Are there structural problems with the size, hours of work, committee rules, length of service, or the two party system dominance or is the problem with the individuals themselves that are elected, their ideologies, work ethic, or inappropriate response to lobbyists and campaign funding?

As was stated in the beginning of this book, reelection is the nature of the beast, and so is dedication to party caucus. Making congress a part time job and creating term limits would basically nullify the benefits outlined below and bring the position back to more of a privilege to serve the American people. Then there is the question of size of Congress, 535 members seems like overkill to me. Do we really need two chambers in Congress? Have times changed that our forefathers didn't anticipate, i.e., email, telecoms, and social media? Could we have one chamber of Congress that reflects a state's population instead of state districting as is done with the members of the House of Representatives?

Salary and Benefits

Prior to 1984, neither members of Congress nor any other federal civil service employee were eligible to pay into Social Security. Members of Congress and other federal employees were covered by a government pension plan called the Civil Service Retirement System (CSRS). In 1983, the Social Security Act was amended and now requires federal employees hired after 1983 to participate in Social Security, including members of Congress regardless of when they first entered Congress. This new retirement plan for federal workers was a result of the Federal Employees' Retirement System (FERS) Act of 1986.

Members of Congress receive retirement and health benefits under the same plans available to other federal employees and they become vested after five years of full participation. Members elected since 1984 are now covered by FERS. Federal employees and those members elected prior to 1984 were covered by the Civil Service Retirement System (CSRS). In 1984 all federal employees and members were given the option of remaining with CSRS or switching to FERS. Members of Congress under FERS contribute 1.3 percent of their salary into the FERS retirement plan and pay 6.2 percent of their salary in Social Security taxes.

Federal employees and members of Congress are not eligible for a pension until they reach the age of 50, but only if they've completed 20 years of service. Members are eligible at any age after completing 25 years of service or after they reach the age of 62. The amount of a congressperson's pension, as with other government employees, depends on the years of service and the average of the highest 3 years of his or her salary.

Salary and benefits for members of Congress is not my biggest concern except for the fact that they are not fulltime, 40 hour per week workers. Even our government SESs work fulltime 40 hour weeks without the "breaks" taken by members of Congress. Our forefathers envisioned the Congress as part time, where it was made up of farmers, businessmen, lawyers, teachers, doctors, and preachers who all had careers and full time jobs at home. Even though the majority of members today are wealthy on their own, it has become a career to be a member of Congress. Would making the Congress a part-time body enable members to spend more time with their constituents outside of Washington D.C. and "K" Street? Or is the whole game simply just a case of money, money for the sake of reelection, vote buying for the sake of reelection. It seems like the country is being sold out.

Campaign Funding Reform

Candidates, parties, political action committees, and other special interest groups spent more than $7 billion on the 2012 election, according to a final tally by the Federal Election Commission. That's the most ever spent on U.S. elections, and surpasses the $5.3 billion spent in 2008. It should be unethical to spend this much money on political campaigning verses spending it on more worthwhile charities or private investment in public works.

The Supreme Court has ruled that campaign funds and lobbying are matters of free speech. I guess "money does talk" after all. If limits or caps cannot be put back in place to limit the amount that can be spent on a political party or candidate perhaps we need to level the playing field through public financing of campaigns. Eliminating what the government wastes on earmarks and other special interests through lobbyists would more than compensate for the public funding of campaigns. With public financing of campaigns we could also require states to permit independents or third-party candidates the same rights to ballot access and public financing.

Maybe money doesn't always talk in elections, just equal time in public broadcasting might make a difference. After all, back in June 2014, Eric Cantor, House Majority Leader, spent $1 million in the weeks leading up to the primary election in Virginia, when his primary opponent had only $100,000. Eric Cantor was defeated by Dave Brat, a college economics professor. This was a rare overturn and perhaps a model for campaign change. Politicians think they need large sums of money to campaign for election. Currently they get most of it from wealthy donors and business and special interests such as lobbyists. Contributors generally expect paybacks in some form, such as favorable legislation, earmarks, government contracts, or government jobs. The only way to stop this is for candidates to not payback.

Ordinary citizens who want to serve in public office may not have access to vast amounts of campaign funds. There is a Fair Elections Now Act that has been drafted that would give candidates $4 for every $1 they receive in small contributions so that ordinary people can fund a candidate. There is also the Government by the People Act that has similar components.

Lobbying

Lobbying in the federal government has increased over the past several decades. Lobbying is an attempt to influence decisions made by officials in the government. Many times these officials are legislators or members of regulatory agencies in an effort to accomplish special interest policies.

Lobbying can also be used to serve private interests and can also be used to defend others interests against unfairness or minority interests.

Paying a policy maker for their vote or decision is illegal, as is providing gifts and other amenities. Then there is the "revolving door" where many former lobbyists are hired into high level government jobs that may appear to be a conflict of interest. Other examples of the revolving door are when the government hires industry professionals for their private sector experience and their influence within corporations that the government is attempting to regulate or do business with. Industry also hires people out of government positions to gain personal access to government officials and seek favorable legislation/regulation and government contracts.

Timothy P. Carney, *Senior Political Columnist,* The Washington Examiner, identified many former lobbyists that have or are working for the current and former administrations. More than you could have imagined. Lobbyists have been instrumental in changing current law with respect to deregulating FDA oversight of the drug compounding businesses that resulted in contaminated drugs sold to some physician offices and the repeal of the Glass-Steagall Act in 1999, a former law that was created as a banking reform following the Great Depression by separating commercial banking from investment banking. Lobbyists also stand up for citizen rights and other civil and humane causes. Many lobbyist are deregistering as lobbyists even though they are still employed with the same company. This makes it appear that lobbying is reducing but this may not be the case. According to Roll Call's Kate Ackley, "total lobbying tab for 2011 and 2012", she concluded at the time that much "of the work influencing government takes place in the shadows, outside of the view of public disclosures."

Earmarking Legislation

Last winter I was in line at a grocery store to buy lunch meat and a man also in line and I were talking about college and our majors. I said I had majored in political science. The man said that "ever since a U.S. House of Representative banned earmarks" — spending projects that members of congress were allowed to put into appropriation legislation to direct funds and projects to their districts – "Congress hasn't been able to pass any legislation." Maybe he was right because there is no more wheeling and dealing in the form of earmarks. Or maybe not passing some of the legislation is a good thing. It is not the quantity of bills passed but the content of the legislation. For starters, Americans just want legislation and funding that would help grow the economy and put Americans back to work.

Requiring both chambers of Congress to introduce and pass legislation has become a real problem. Bills passed by one chamber are not being considered in the other chamber. This is congressional gridlock and a refusal of some in Congress to do their jobs. At least they were able to muster up the continuing resolution to continue to fund the government by the end of September 2014 before they went on another "break" to campaign back at home.

That aside, Congress needs to be able to compromise for the better good and for what is right verses making self-interest decisions based on horse trading. That is what is supposed to happen, at least in theory. While some earmarked projects may be worthwhile, I'm not sure they are the highest priority projects for federal investment. Earmarks can cause inaction on more important legislation. Apparently, the $60 billion Hurricane Sandy aid package that passed the Senate on December 29, 2012, was loaded with earmarks that caused the legislation to not pass the House in a timely manner. Apparently the bill contained billions unrelated to the damage wrought by the hurricane, according to an analysis by the independent watchdog group Taxpayers for Common Sense, including provisions like $150 million for fisheries as far away as Alaska or $821 million for harbor dredging that could benefit Mississippi River towns like St. Louis.

Bicameral Structure of Congress/Term Limits

Creating term limits removes the incentive to be reelected as the only goal for serving in Congress, and therefore creates less pressure from lobbyists and campaign donations to control politicians and policy. The problem with term limits is that good congresspersons at some point cannot be reelected! Perhaps we could allow a petition to be signed to allow an exception to the term limits?

If a member is constantly running for reelection and buying votes for reelection they will not be effective and focused on the job at hand. Our founding fathers provided that members of the U.S. House of Representatives be elected by and represent small geographically defined districts within each state. Senators, on the other hand, in theory, are elected by and represent all voters of their state. Maybe that is where we have gotten to, the need to consider national interests in Congress instead of local concerns. If so, where does that leave the role of House of Representatives?

All members of the House are up for election every two years. So, in effect, they are always running for election and always subject to the lobbyists to ensure reelection. The two year election cycle was supposed to ensure that members would maintain personal contact with their local constituents and be better able to advocate for them in Congress.

Senators are elected for six-year terms and therefore may be less focused on reelection and more likely to be concerned with national priorities.

I don't think our forefathers anticipated the impact of constant reelection every two years nor the tremendous rise in lobbying as we have today. I know they feared political faction as a destructive force against democracy. I am also not convinced that this number of representatives and senators is not overkill and part of the reason decisions cannot be made in Congress. Communications have changed drastically since the drafting of the U.S. Constitution so localities shouldn't be a factor anymore, or are they? This seems extreme but, what if we eliminated the House of Representatives and either increased the number of senators based on state population or retained the two senators per state? It would eliminate redistricting and gerrymandering problems because senators do not have districts. I think I like term limits for both chambers with the ability to petition an exception if the candidate is determined "by the people" to be a valued member of Congress. What do you think?

However, what was the purpose in the U.S. Constitution of creating a bicameral structure in Congress, dividing Congress into two chambers, requiring both chambers to approve legislation? Was it a "check and balance" to prevent tyranny by one chamber? Or was it modeled after the two chamber British Parliament structure? Or was it "The Great

Compromise" as it has been called to appease both small and large states? Or are they redundant institutions?

Max Baucus, Chairman of the Senate Finance Committee, announced on April 23, 2013, that he is retiring from the senate and is not seeking a 7th term of office in 2014. He declared himself "unconstrained" by electoral politics for the first time since coming to Congress in 1975, according to Richard Rubin of Bloomberg News. Without concern for reelection, he now has more time now to focus on tax reform. Campaigning and drafting major legislation are both time consuming and campaigning would be a distraction to drafting major legislation. I am not sure what he was able to accomplish with regard to tax reform but you can see the impact on governance when reelection is right around the corner. In addition, there are many members currently in Congress who have spent at least half of their lives in Congress.

Electoral College

The United States Electoral College is the system that officially elects the President and Vice President of the United States every four years. The President and Vice President are not elected directly by the voters based on a popular vote, one person one vote basis, as in the case with Congress. Instead, they are elected by "electors" who are chosen by popular vote on a state-by-state basis. Each state appoints its electors on a winner-take-all basis, based on the statewide popular vote.

A state's number of electors equals the number of representatives and senators the state has in the U.S. Congress, except for smaller states that have just one House representative are allowed 3 electoral candidates. The Electoral College system was supposedly created to achieve a more balanced outcome of national elections for president and vice president by reducing dominance of states with large population. The candidate who wins the popular vote in each congressional district wins the electoral vote from that congressional district, and the candidate who wins the entire state receives the state's two remaining electoral votes. Therefore, if the bicameral structure of Congress was changed to remove congressional districts, the national election process would have to be altered. The Electoral College system allows the possibility of a candidate actually losing the nationwide popular vote, but being elected president by the electoral vote. This has happened four times in U.S. history with the elections of 1824, 1876, 1888, and 2000. In these four cases the winner of the election did not carry the popular vote. You may say why bother to vote. The Electoral College may decrease the advantage that a political party campaign might gain when encouraging voter to turn out, except in "swing states" where Republican and Democratic candidates both have a chance of winning. The winner-take-all manner of allocating a state's electors may decrease the importance of minor parties.

The Two Party System - Make Room for the Independents and Others

The gridlock currently in Congress has made the institution ineffective and virtually obsolete. That in itself threatens democracy as we know it. When the people cannot be heard or listened to through their representatives because party leadership in Congress has become excessively controlling to members and has made this Congress the most unpopular in history. What does this tell us? Americans are party weary. Independents, of which I am one, usually have views of both parties as we know them today. Independents can be of any political persuasion, but the term most commonly refers to politicians or voters who hold centrist views that incorporate facets of both Democratic and Republican ideology. Many now seem to "label" themselves as independents more so than in the past.

What if there was no two party system, and the speaker of the house and committee chairpersons and members were more bipartisanly selected? The concern is perhaps that too much power is vested in these officials. What if you ran for Congress and then found out that your views and legislation cannot be heard? That would deter the best of us from running for public office. Our founding fathers didn't intend for American politics to be partisan. There is no mention of political parties in the U.S. Constitution.

In the 1790s the Federalist Party and the Democratic-Republican Party emerged into a two party-type system due to differing views on federal government powers. Consensus was eventually reached and party politics ended in 1816. Partisan politics was revived in 1829 with the split of the Democratic-Republican Party into the Jacksonian Democrats and the Whig Party. In the 1850s, the Jacksonian Democrats evolved into the Democratic Party and the Whig Party became the Republican Party as we know them today.

The Parties Verses the People, How to Turn Republicans and Democrats into Americans is a book written by a former Oklahoma Congressman Mickey Edwards. This book provides great insight into partisan dysfunction in Congress and his proposed ways to correct this problem. Mr. Edwards proposes taking away party control over access to the ballot and redistricting, ways to establish a nonpartisan congressional leadership and nonpartisan congressional committees, and equal party representation on the Rules Committee in the House of Representatives.

The U.S. Constitution allows the House of Representatives to choose their Speaker but it doesn't outline the role of the Speaker or how he or she should be selected. He thinks that it would help if the Speaker could be voted on by secret ballot to avoid fear of retaliation by party leaders. The requirements for election should be designed to make strict partisanship almost impossible.

Party leaders have complete control over appointments to congressional committees. In establishing nonpartisan congressional committees, Mr. Edwards states that "One way to start is to ensure each committee has a chair from the majority party and a vice chairman from the minority. Second, change the way committee members are appointed." In making the Rules Committee in the House of Representatives bipartisan, Mr. Edwards suggests that both political parties should be equally represented.

According to Article 1, Section 4, of the Constitution, the authority to regulate the time, place, and manner of federal elections is up to each State, unless Congress legislates otherwise. Each State has its own ballot access laws to determine who may appear on ballots and who may not. Maybe it is time to rethink this thing. Mr. Edwards proposes that we eliminate the ability of political parties to determine who can run in a general election by creating new systems of open integrated primaries. Candidates for an office, regardless of party, appear on the same ballot, and every registered voter may participate. The top two candidates, regardless of party, run against each other in the general election. This is currently done in Washington, California, and Louisiana.

Mr. Edwards proposes taking away the parties' control over redistricting, otherwise known as gerrymandering, when congressional districts are shaped based on partisan advantage. He proposes removing the power to redistrict from the state legislatures or governors. He believes there is value in independent, nonpartisan redistricting commissions.

Health Care

National health care expenditures nearly doubled from 2000 to 2011, from $1,377.2 billion to $2,700.7 billion according to Government Executive. "If the government could help in controlling health care costs, it would not only save dollars spent by health insurance companies, it would make it more affordable for each individual to secure good health care." It suggested that the government could help the health care market by collecting and publishing basic price data.

I concur that unreasonable health care costs are the cause for Americans not being able to afford health care, regardless of the health care system they chose. You can get an MRI cheaper from the small MRI office down the street verses the cost of an MRI in a large hospital. So what does that tell you? Where are our antitrust laws when it comes to the pharmaceutical companies and the heath-care market?

I do not believe universal health care is the role for the federal government as reflected in the Affordable Care Act. The federal government role should be in regulating health care costs and perhaps expanding the existing Medicaid system to those who can't afford health care, such as persons in Appalachia and our inner cities. We haven't figured out how to continue to fund the entitlement programs currently in effect. Requiring payroll contributions based on actual income levels without a cap might be a start. However, it doesn't make sense that we would add more economic burden in the form of subsidies to the federal government without first trying to fix the cause of why health care is not affordable. The President and Congress have done nothing to reform the entitlement programs and the U.S. tax code. Once the Obamacare legislation passed Congress they had years to try to fix it and not wait until the eleventh hour to hold the country hostage with no specific recommendations for changes to the Affordable Care Act.

We were forced into paying social security and Medicare with much the same congressional disagreement at the time. We need to fix the fate of those programs to be able to sustain themselves. Adding another social program is questionable, especially after seeing the role out of the program and the costs associated with it, let alone the implications to those who had insurance and the businesses that had health benefits for their employees, which in many instances have been dropped and employees now working less hours to escape the impact to business costs under the regulations. I wish we would have just expanded Medicare to cover those with preexisting conditions and Medicaid for those who cannot afford health care. It seems it would have been less expensive and less disruptive to jobs and our economy. We may need to face the same problem with the VA. Is it cost effective to have VA medical centers or just focus on health costs in general and have veterans use our existing health care system? I do not know. Someone would have to do the numbers, but we do know that veterans would get immediate service and not have sit on imaginary waiting lists.

Social Security and Medicare

Social Security and Medicare are paid for by income and payroll taxes by most employees, with some exceptions. Social Security and Medicare taxes will take 6.2 percent and 1.45 percent of each paycheck. Employers also match the employee's contribution. Of all of the Social Security taxes (known as FICA taxes) collected, 85 cents of every dollar goes into the Old Age and Survivors part of the Social Security trust fund and 15 cents goes into the Disability part. Supplemental Security Income, which is an income-based disability program, is not funded through the

FICA taxes, but through general tax revenues. There is an annual limit on the amount of income subject to social security tax. Once a worker earns $117,000 and has contributed to social security, further income earnings are exempt from further withholding. Sounds similar to the cap on income tax. I wonder why?

According to the *2013 Annual Report of the Board of Trustees of the Federal Old-Age and Survivors Insurance and Federal Disability Insurance Trust Funds* given to Congress by the Social Security Board of Trustees, Social Security will be able to pay promised benefits through 2033. After that time, FICA tax revenues will only provide enough to pay 77 percent of benefits. The Disability Insurance Trust Fund reserves become depleted in 2016 and the Old Age and Survivors Insurance Trust Fund reserves run out in 2035.

Some say that Social Security is sustainable because of its widespread applicability as a dedicated tax source. Not so with pension plans and 401(k) balances. Social Security is based on a dedicated payroll tax base and annual benefit payouts that will hopefully grow at the same pace. However, as the share of the working-age population shrinks, the allocation of benefits may be larger than the growth of taxable wages. What if we raised the cap on income subject to social security and Medicare taxes? Seems logical to me but I am no expert. If we have Medicare why not apply it to all, regardless of age or a precondition illness, and get rid of Obamacare. Some say Medicare would hold administrative health care costs down tremendously.

Medicaid gives people with little or no medical insurance who are low-income, elderly, or disabled access to medical benefits. Funded jointly with the federal government, states determine eligibility requirements and services provided. If we already use this program to cover those who cannot afford health care why not use it for all low income folks that can't afford health care instead of Obamacare?

Some believe we need to cut these programs so the government can supposedly reverse the government's debt, but I am not convinced. They will just spend more on something else. We must have a safety net for those who need it. I think the average amount 401(k) amount saved is not enough. Pension plans have been going broke, like the city of Detroit, and companies file bankruptcy, employees lose their pensions, and new companies do not even offer pension plans.

Welfare and Unemployment Reform

In Chapter 2 we discussed the fraud that exists in the Welfare Program. Now more people are on long term unemployment than we have seen in years, if not a decade. We just commemorated 50 years since President Johnson started the "War on Poverty." But where has it gotten us? I fear the Great Recession, years of outsourcing jobs and unemployment have caused unemployment to be the new welfare system.

The Personal Responsibility and Work Opportunity Reconciliation Act of 1996, known as the "The Welfare Reform Act", is the federal government's reform of the welfare system. Under the Welfare Reform Act, recipients are required to find jobs within two years of first receiving welfare payments; most recipients are allowed to receive welfare payments for a total of no more than five years; and the states are allowed to establish "family caps" that prevent mothers of babies born while the mother is already on welfare from receiving additional benefits.

According to the Brookings Institute, the nationwide welfare caseload declined by about 60 percent between 1994 and 2004. Census Bureau data shows that between 1993 and 2000, the percentage of low-income, single mothers with a job grew from 58 percent to nearly 75 percent.

However, according to a report from the non-partisan Congressional Research Service (CRS), more than 80, often overlapping, welfare programs made up the largest part of the U.S. federal government budget, costing taxpayers roughly $1.03 trillion in 2011. CRS found that exclusively federal spending on 83 federal programs that provide benefits or services to people with low incomes equaled approximately $746 billion, while required state contributions to same programs amounted to another $283 billion for a total cost to taxpayers of $1.03 trillion.

The 83 federal programs examined by the CRS included only "means-tested" programs, meaning that their benefits are paid only to households or individuals with incomes at or below federal poverty levels. They do not include programs to assist veterans, or entitlement programs, like Social Security and Medicare, to which people contribute through payroll deductions or monthly premiums.

By comparison, the CRS noted that in 2011, the federal budget expenditure for Social Security was $725 billion, $480 billion for Medicare and $540 billion for non-war related defense programs. As mentioned previously, we know there is a lot of fraud in the Welfare and Social Security Disability programs. This should be the focus as well to stop the costs of these programs.

So we need take this farther. Force mandatory work for program coverage. This could result in support for local businesses or government that would otherwise have to pay for these services. An example would be performing field work, and other undesirable work, that farmers and others are having trouble finding workers that want the jobs. There is also nonprofit and community work that could be performed. This approach would train the unemployed in new skills for a better future and stay off government programs.

Mothers with children should receive day care or preschool while on welfare so they can work. This provides two benefits into one. Consolidate all these programs and focus on job growth, it is more humane and more cost effective.

Billionaire investor Warren Buffett is the world's fourth-richest person and has committed almost all his wealth to charity. As Warren Buffet stated at a Georgetown University event, *"We have learned to turn out lots of goods and services, but we haven't learned as well how to have everybody share in the bounty. The obligation of a society as prosperous as ours is to figure out how nobody gets left too far behind."*

The War on Poverty involves the need for economic growth and jobs that sufficiently pay enough to sustain families. Higher education is increasingly expensive and training programs are insufficient or ineffective. The drastically inequitable economy was the precipitous to the Great Depression. All these play a role in our war against poverty. As we discussed earlier, corporate taxes need to be lowered along with creating other business incentives to keep businesses from outsourcing jobs overseas. Making income taxes fair based on income, and using the revenues to create jobs, internships, and other training related initiates and at the same time improving our infrastructure, energy independence, our educational system, and barriers facing some minorities. Subsidizing the poor without forcing them out of their circumstances with job training, day care, work experience will not solve the problem.

CHAPTER FOUR
WHERE'S MY WHITE PICKET FENCE?

We have discussed corporate and private interest influence over government policies for the past several decades, including the tax code and the deregulation of many industries, including the airline and trucking industries. As a result of deregulation, businesses merged, businesses went bankrupt, and with them went their employees' jobs and or salary levels, and their pensions. We also discussed the corporate outsourcing of jobs overseas, causing further job loss and insecurity to Americans. The administration policies in the 1980s and 1990s supported the growth in real estate with the belief that owning a home was a good investment, the American Dream.

The American Dream for Sale

Under encouragement by several Administrations, legislation was enacted in 1980, eliminating the ceiling on mortgage interest rates. In 1982, legislation was enacted that permitted state banks to sell adjustable rate mortgages, equity stripping loans, and 100 percent financing where no down payment was required. In 1984, another law was enacted that allowed federally-chartered and regulated financial institutions to invest in mortgage-backed securities. Banks were allowed to sell mortgages to Wall Street banks which created a secondary mortgage market that vastly expanded. Then in 1999, Congress passes the Gramm–Leach–Bliley Act, otherwise known as the Financial Services Modernization Act, repealing parts of the Glass-Steagall Act that was enacted in 1933 following the Great Depression to rein in the financial industry from gambling with our bank deposits and separate commercial and investment banking. The new law removed regulatory barriers between banks, securities companies, and insurers so they could sell each other's financial products.

Meanwhile, from the 1980s until 2001, home prices rose in step with inflation. And then in 2001 home prices went through the roof, so to speak. The housing price growth that started in 2001 was due to the Federal Reserve Chairman lowering interest rates and the mortgage industry gearing up when people could easily attain loans with little or no documentation, loans that came to be known as "liar loans" under this new mortgage playing field. With it went the 30 year fixed mortgage, just not enough money in it anymore for the banks! The quantity of loans was where the money was, along with higher fees and eventually higher interest rates. Some lenders looked the other way and others repackaged the loans into toxic investments that managed to receive AAA credit ratings. Thus setting up for the perfect storm.

A new risky subprime mortgage practice goes into full effect in America. The practice in one where risky loans with high interest rates and fees are sold to buyers that would not qualify for a prime mortgage. These mortgages would later be packaged and sold, eventually finding their way to Wall Street. They offered adjustable mortgages to people who had no chance of affording the mortgage after the rate adjusted up. They lent to people with too much debt. They wrote "interest only" loans that ensured the loan balance would be greater than the price of the house in three years. They levied penalties and changed terms at the last minute, unknown to buyers. Loan documents were altered and income falsified by lenders. Independent brokers originating the loans really didn't care if the mortgage loan would be paid back or not. They would collect their fee and move the risk on down the line to the mortgage broker who bundled the loans and sold them to investors.

Incomes had been stagnant or fallen for years but U.S. home prices continue to rise drastically. The feeling in the industry and the government was that real estate would continue to appreciate. However, massive defaults on home mortgages were inevitable due to the eventual impact of the adjustable rate loans and the risky loan approvals based on questionable income and debt information falsely documented by loan officials. The housing bubble burst when borrowers defaulted on loans and the value of the securities sold to Wall Street fell. The financial institutions did not have adequate capital reserves to back up all the financial commitments.

The American Nightmare

As home values declined, home owners became "underwater" on their mortgages. Their homes were now worth less than their mortgage balance. That made it difficult to refinance or sell their property. Banks foreclosed on property owners, and many were wrongly foreclosed on even though they were current on their mortgage payments.

In September 2008, Lehman Brothers and then American International Group (AIG) collapsed, the stock market fell, 401 (k) retirement accounts were lost, and unemployment hit all-time highs. Income inequality was at extremes. The threat of bankruptcy in our largest financial institutions and many of our citizens was on the horizon. According to a report released by the National Bankruptcy Research Center, personal bankruptcy filings were up 34 percent in January 2009 as compared to January 2008. However, bankruptcy laws treat personal bankruptcy differently from corporate bankruptcy. My understanding is that mortgages can't be refinanced and student loans can't be written off but corporations may be able to eventually "reorganize their assets" and start over.

Among the largest companies that filed bankruptcy were Lehman Brothers Holdings Inc. Its collapse was the largest corporate bankruptcy in U.S. history, involving debt amounting to $613 billion and assets worth $639 billion. Washington Mutual, Inc., then the largest savings and loan association in the U.S., was the largest bank failure in U.S. history. Corporate bankruptcy leads to layoffs, unemployment, reduced consumer spending and overall slower economic growth. But somehow those who were bailed out still managed to receive huge bonuses. As the story goes, the rich just got richer.

Government bailouts were necessary in 2008 to keep the financial system operating in fear of creating a depression. Bailouts also went to General Motors and others outside the financial system. The Emergency Economic Stabilization Act of 2008 was signed into law creating a $700 billion Troubled Asset Relief Program (TARP) to purchase failing bank assets.

TARP was unpopular with the public who did not want to bail out Wall Street with tax payer money. Individuals were not bailed out when they lost their 401(k) retirement funds or lost their jobs and pensions when corporations "reorganized their assets". We do need commercial banks and traditional savings and loan banks to provide a safe place to store our money and we need banks to provide loans to those who will spur the economy in consumer spending or small business enterprises. These type of banks deserve to be covered by deposit insurance, the Federal Deposit Insurance Corporation (FDIC) as we know it today. The question was, and still is, why not separate these banks from risky investment banks and remove the possibility that a failure could endanger the financial system, and better able criminal behavior to be prosecuted without the fear of too big to prosecute.

Apparently, more assistance came from the government in addition to the TARP program. In an excerpt cited below from an article by Bloomberg Markets Magazine, November 28, 2011, "The Fed had committed $7.77 trillion as of March 2009 to rescuing the financial system, more than half the value of everything produced in the U.S. that year".

Apparently, the Federal Reserve and the big banks tried to keep details of the huge bailout a secret. The big banks became even bigger. The bankers lobbied against government regulations.

But now the banks do not want to "write down" the old loans and refinance loans for those who are underwater on their loans. However, refinancing these loans seems to be the right thing to do for homeowners since we bailed out the banks when they went under!

N. E. Parks

Too Big to Fail, Too Big to Prosecute

Has capitalism gone too far? The idea that one sector has so much power over the economy that if they fall the whole global economy collapses. Apparently this financial industry has grown even bigger than it was before the recession. I have said I am no economist and I certainly know even less about the stock market. Common sense tells me that this is a scary situation, especially for all those that now rely on their 401(k) savings for retirement security. Can we have an even larger crash in the future if these firms are allowed to operate with no caps on their size and amount of risk? Apparently a few hedge funds realized that the securities were "toxic" and made money when the market collapsed on "credit default swaps." When commercial banks can invest in risky derivatives with depositor funds and without much regulation, how could the federal government really secure all depositor funds if lost? When these banks bought up other banks they became too big to fail.

Many say the cause of the stock market crash of 1929 was "overvalued" stocks. According to Investopedia, overvalued stock is a stock with a current price that is not justified by its earnings outlook or price/earnings (P/E) ratio and, therefore, is expected to drop in price. Before the stock market crash of 1929 there were also many new banks starting into the business without sufficient regulation to determine the minimum capital required of a bank or any rules on the amount of reserves that could be loaned. There was also a rapid expansion in the U.S. stock market preceding the crash. The stock market crash in 1929 was followed by a three-year bear market and the Great Depression. It took decades for the stock market to recover.

Franklin Roosevelt was elected president at the end of 1933. He created what is known as the New Deal that would create programs, policy, and agencies to revive industry and agriculture and create jobs. Among the agencies created were the Agricultural Adjustment Administration (AAA), the Public Works Administration (PWA), the Civilian Conservations Corps (CCC), and the Tennessee Valley Authority (TVA). Policy reform directed at the financial system included enactment of the Glass-Stegall Act in 1933. As mentioned previously, this act separated commercial and the investment banks. The Federal Deposit Insurance Corporation (FDIC) was established to insure bank deposits and the Securities and Exchange Commission (SEC) was formed to protect against stock market fraud. The "second new deal" came in 1935 and included the Social Security Act (which for the first time provided Americans with unemployment, disability, and pensions for old age) and the Works Progress Administration. However, it wasn't until the early 1940s, with the military buildup in the United States as it entered

World War ll, that the U.S. economy improved due to the revitalization of industry due to the demand for war related materials.

Interestingly, the stock market crash of 1987 was believed by some analysts to have been caused by large stock market computer trading. Big investment companies ordered extremely large stock trades through computers. The market failed to manage the sudden and extremely high volume of sells and it lacked liquidity. As a result, the Chicago Mercantile Exchange and the New York Stock Exchange (NYSE) together introduced the "circuit breaker" mechanism. This system was installed in these two exchanges to supposedly prevent any further stock market crashes. The market would automatically halt if the Dow had a major fall and during this period no trade could be carried out in these two exchanges. If the Dow fell 250 points or more, the market would stop its trading for an hour. If the fall had been for more than 400 points then the market would halt for two hours.

Many say the Dot Com Bubble Burst is what caused the 2000 stock market crash. The years 1992-2000 were favorable for the stock market. The dot com boom involved services such as information generation and sharing, information technology, consultation, education, research and development, financial planning, and other knowledge-based services. Another probable reason for the 2000 stock market crash was the overvaluation of the stocks.

When the stock market crashed in 2000, there was a shift in dollars going away from the stock market into housing. To further fuel the housing bubble there was plenty of cheap money available for new loans at the heels of the economic recession. The Federal Reserve and banks praised the housing market for helping to create wealth and provide a secured asset that people could borrow money to help the economy grow. Now we know the rest of the story.

Following the 2008 financial crisis, the Dodd-Frank Wall Street Reform Act into law in 2010. Dodd-Frank proposed many areas of regulation but it didn't go as far as the Glass-Stegall Act to separate commercial and the investment banks. It did create the Volker Rule which bans banks from using or owning hedge funds for the banks' own profit. Banks can use hedge funds for their customers only. Banks have until July 21, 2015 to implement the rule. But will it go far enough to avoid another stock market crash and bailout? What do we do with the savings accumulated if this occurs? There is no money in savings and loans interest. A safer bet might be to put it under our mattresses.

Recently, on 60 Minutes, we found out that the stock market was rigged. Trades being made by computers that were so fast that the transactions could not be recorded. The way I understood the 60 minutes piece was that insiders see your order and play or front run your trade and then sell it back to you while driving up the price.

High frequency trading is what it is called and gaming the system through miles of fiber optic cable. I give up, what is going on? If this is how the United States stock market, the most iconic market in global capitalism, is run I am concerned.

According to the Hill, Eric Holder, U.S. Attorney General, stated "I am concerned that the size of some of these institutions becomes so large that it does become difficult for us to prosecute them when we are hit with indications that if you do prosecute, if you do bring a criminal charge, it will have a negative impact on the national economy, perhaps even the world economy."

Federal Reserve System

The Federal Reserve System is the central banking system of the United States. It was established with the enactment of the Federal Reserve Act in 1913, following a series of financial panics. The roles and responsibilities of the Federal Reserve System have expanded over time. Apparently the Great Depression in 1929 was a major factor leading to changes in the system.

Did the Federal Reserve fulfill its mission to control inflation and avoid the Great Recession? We did not escape from the recession. My grocery bill indicates a rise in inflation even though the official stats report otherwise. More than a quarter of the unemployed workers in the United States say they have been out of work for at least a year, and that does not count those who have given up looking, since they are no longer counted as unemployed. That is down from nearly a third at the peak of the recession, but far higher than it had ever been before the recession that began in 2007.

The Federal Reserve Chairperson is responsible for preventing inflation and recession. Part of the Fed chair's job is to oversee the largest bank holding companies, assuring their safety and soundness and implementing dozens of new regulations under the 2010 Dodd-Frank Act that could crimp their profits. The Fed is a direct supervisor of New York-based Citigroup and annually tests it and other large banks' durability against financial stress.

We have many oversight agencies to watch out for our financial system. It consists of the Federal Deposit Insurance Corporation (FDIC), Securities and Exchange Commission (The SEC), Office of the Comptroller of the Currency (OCC), Consumer Financial Protection Bureau (CFPB), U.S. Commodity Futures Trading Commission (CFTC), Federal Reserve System (The Fed) and (the Treasury) U.S. Department of the Treasury.

Maybe we need to rethink this thing. Is this another case of too many regulators without any accountability? It seems we make everything so complicated. The Federal Reserve's stimulus programs helped corporate America, but they did little to help improve the lives of most Americans.

CHAPTER FIVE

LIFE, LIBERTY, AND THE PURSUIT OF HAPPINESS

"**Life, Liberty and the pursuit of Happiness**" is a phrase in the United States Declaration of Independence cited below. The phrase outlines three "unalienable rights" which the Declaration says has been given to all human beings by their Creator, and for which governments are created to protect. "We hold these truths to be self-evident, that all men are created equal, that they are endowed by their Creator with certain unalienable Rights, that among these are Life, Liberty and the pursuit of Happiness."

According to Wikipedia, this has been called "one of the best-known sentences in the English language, containing the most potent and consequential words in American history. The passage came to represent a moral standard to which the United States should strive."

The declaration of Independence states further "That to secure these rights, Governments are instituted among Men, deriving their just powers from the consent of the governed......" Thus declaring representation of the people as an alternative to monarchy and hereditary rule. The balance of power outlined in the U.S. Constitution was designed to prevent tyranny, a form of government with an absolute dictator that is not restricted by a constitution or laws.

IN CONGRESS, JULY 4, 1776

The unanimous Declaration of the thirteen united States of America

When in the Course of human events it becomes necessary for one people to dissolve the political bands which have connected them with another and to assume among the powers of the earth, the separate and equal station to which the Laws of Nature and of Nature's God entitle them, a decent respect to the opinions of mankind requires that they should declare the causes which impel them to the separation.

We hold these truths to be self-evident, that all men are created equal, that they are endowed by their Creator with certain unalienable Rights, that among these are Life, Liberty and the pursuit of Happiness. — That to secure these rights, Governments are instituted among Men, deriving their just powers from the consent of the governed, — That whenever any Form of Government becomes destructive of these ends, it is the Right of the People to alter or to abolish it, and to institute new Government, laying its foundation on such principles and organizing its powers in such form, as to them shall seem most likely to effect their Safety and Happiness. Prudence, indeed, will dictate that Governments long established should not be changed for light and transient causes; and accordingly all experience hath shewn that mankind are more disposed to suffer, while evils are sufferable than to right themselves by abolishing the forms to which they are accustomed. But when a long train of abuses and usurpations, pursuing invariably the same Object evinces a design to reduce them under absolute Despotism, it is their right, it is their duty, to throw off such Government, and to provide new Guards for their future security. — Such has been the patient sufferance of these Colonies; and such is now the necessity which constrains them to alter their former Systems of Government. The history of the present King of Great Britain is a history of repeated injuries and usurpations, all having in direct object the establishment of an absolute Tyranny over these States. To prove this, let Facts be submitted to a candid world.

He has refused his Assent to Laws, the most wholesome and necessary for the public good.

He has forbidden his Governors to pass Laws of immediate and pressing importance, unless suspended in their operation till his Assent should be obtained; and when so suspended, he has utterly neglected to attend to them.

He has refused to pass other Laws for the accommodation of large districts of people, unless those people would relinquish the right of Representation in the Legislature, a right inestimable to them and formidable to tyrants only.

He has called together legislative bodies at places unusual, uncomfortable, and distant from the depository of their Public Records, for the sole purpose of fatiguing them into compliance with his measures.

He has dissolved Representative Houses repeatedly, for opposing with manly firmness his invasions on the rights of the people.

He has refused for a long time, after such dissolutions, to cause others to be elected, whereby the Legislative Powers, incapable of Annihilation, have returned to the People at large for their exercise; the State remaining in the meantime exposed to all the dangers of invasion from without, and convulsions within.

He has endeavored to prevent the population of these States; for that purpose obstructing the Laws for Naturalization of Foreigners; refusing to pass others to encourage their migrations hither, and raising the conditions of new Appropriations of Lands.

He has obstructed the Administration of Justice by refusing his Assent to Laws for establishing Judiciary Powers.

He has made Judges dependent on his Will alone for the tenure of their offices, and the amount and payment of their salaries.

He has erected a multitude of New Offices, and sent hither swarms of Officers to harass our people and eat out their substance.

He has kept among us, in times of peace, Standing Armies without the Consent of our legislatures.

He has affected to render the Military independent of and superior to the Civil Power.

He has combined with others to subject us to a jurisdiction foreign to our constitution, and unacknowledged by our laws; giving his Assent to their Acts of pretended Legislation:

For quartering large bodies of armed troops among us:

For protecting them, by a mock Trial from punishment for any Murders which they should commit on the Inhabitants of these States:

For cutting off our Trade with all parts of the world:

For imposing Taxes on us without our Consent:

For depriving us in many cases, of the benefit of Trial by Jury:

For transporting us beyond Seas to be tried for pretended offences:

For abolishing the free System of English Laws in a neighboring Province, establishing therein an Arbitrary government, and enlarging its Boundaries so as to render it at once an example and fit instrument for introducing the same absolute rule into these Colonies

For taking away our Charters, abolishing our most valuable Laws and altering fundamentally the Forms of our Governments:

For suspending our own Legislatures, and declaring themselves invested with power to legislate for us in all cases whatsoever.

He has abdicated Government here, by declaring us out of his Protection and waging War against us.

He has plundered our seas, ravaged our coasts, burnt our towns, and destroyed the lives of our people.

He is at this time transporting large Armies of foreign Mercenaries to complete the works of death, desolation, and tyranny, already begun with circumstances of Cruelty & Perfidy scarcely paralleled in the most barbarous ages, and totally unworthy the Head of a civilized nation.

He has constrained our fellow Citizens taken Captive on the high Seas to bear Arms against their Country, to become the executioners of their friends and Brethren, or to fall themselves by their Hands.

He has excited domestic insurrections amongst us, and has endeavored to bring on the inhabitants of our frontiers, the merciless Indian Savages whose known rule of warfare, is an undistinguished destruction of all ages, sexes and conditions.

In every stage of these Oppressions We have petitioned for Redress in the most humble terms: Our repeated Petitions have been answered only by repeated injury. A Prince, whose character is thus marked by every act which may define a Tyrant, is unfit to be the ruler of a free people.

Nor have We been wanting in attentions to our British brethren. We have warned them from time to time of attempts by their legislature to extend an unwarrantable jurisdiction over us. We have reminded them of the circumstances of our emigration and settlement here. We have appealed to their native justice and magnanimity, and we have conjured them by the ties of our common kindred to disavow these usurpations, which would inevitably interrupt our connections and correspondence. They too have been deaf to the voice of justice and of consanguinity. We must, therefore, acquiesce in the necessity, which denounces our Separation, and hold them, as we hold the rest of mankind, Enemies in War, in Peace Friends.

We, therefore, the Representatives of the united States of America, in General Congress, Assembled, appealing to the Supreme Judge of the world for the rectitude of our intentions, do, in the Name, and by Authority of the good People of these Colonies, solemnly publish and declare, That these united Colonies are, and of Right ought to be Free and Independent States, that they are Absolved from all Allegiance to the British Crown, and that all political connection between them and the State of Great Britain, is and ought to be totally dissolved; and that as Free and Independent States, they have full Power to levy War, conclude Peace, contract Alliances, establish Commerce, and to do all other Acts and Things which Independent States may of right do. — And for the support of this Declaration, with a firm reliance on the protection of Divine Providence, we mutually pledge to each other our Lives, our Fortunes, and our sacred Honor.

New Hampshire:

Josiah Bartlett, William Whipple, Matthew Thornton

Massachusetts:

John Hancock, Samuel Adams, John Adams, Robert Treat Paine, Elbridge Gerry

Rhode Island:

Stephen Hopkins, William Ellery

Connecticut:

Roger Sherman, Samuel Huntington, William Williams, Oliver Wolcott

New York:

William Floyd, Philip Livingston, Francis Lewis, Lewis Morris

New Jersey:

Richard Stockton, John Witherspoon, Francis Hopkinson, John Hart, Abraham Clark

Pennsylvania:

Robert Morris, Benjamin Rush, Benjamin Franklin, John Morton, George Clymer, James Smith, George Taylor, James Wilson, George Ross

Delaware:

Caesar Rodney, George Read, Thomas McKean

Maryland:

Samuel Chase, William Paca, Thomas Stone, Charles Carroll of Carrollton

Virginia:

George Wythe, Richard Henry Lee, Thomas Jefferson, Benjamin Harrison, Thomas Nelson, Jr., Francis Lightfoot Lee, Carter Braxton

North Carolina:

William Hooper, Joseph Hewes, John Penn

South Carolina:

Edward Rutledge, Thomas Heyward, Jr., Thomas Lynch, Jr., Arthur Middleton

Georgia:

Button Gwinnett, Lyman Hall, George Walton

Taking Back America

This is not the America I grew up in. The America I grew up in punished you if you lied, cheated or stole, we played kick the can until dark but we did not grow up to ignore our responsibilities— to do what was right and fair— not kick them down the road, we didn't bully other children and we respected our elders, and we looked up to the President and Congress because we knew they had our national security and welfare in mind.

Political and economic situations have only deteriorated further with the sequestration and government furloughs, the government shutdown, the debt ceiling can kicked down the road, Obamacare rollout leading to the cancellation of hundreds of thousands of health insurance plans and cost to employers impact employee benefits and hiring, border surge of illegal immigrants, ISIS beheadings, terrorists and other criminals released from prison, U.S. companies continue to move overseas, increase in 3-year visas for college graduates to come to work in the U.S. taking American jobs, substantive unemployment and under employment continues, more school shootings, continued increase in college tuition and heath care costs, executive orders that circumvent the U. S. Congress and the U.S. Constitution, the Secretary of Defense resigns, another year passes without an appropriations bill, and the national deficit rises to 18 trillion dollars and counting.

My mother always told me, "Sometimes things need to get worse before they can get better." I do believe it is time for change and that change will occur for the better good. That is why I decided to write this book. We cannot continue to make laws and decisions that go against the

American people's best interest. I have identified some opportunities to make changes in our federal government's role, programs, and operations and potential reforms to the congressional political structure and policies and our financial institutions as many have done before me.

We cannot leave this mess for our children to try to clean up. This is our mess to clean up. Democrats and Republicans won't be able to clean the mess and it doesn't matter which political party controls the House and the Senate chambers. It is going to take a common cause, a vision, and purpose, similar to that our founding fathers faced when deciding to separate from Great Britain, and strong leadership of the kind we saw in George Washington, Thomas Jefferson, Theodore Roosevelt, and Abraham Lincoln. The common cause is saving America. The secret to taking back America has been in our midst all along buried in the Declaration of Independence; *Life, liberty, and the pursuit of happiness.* I believe this is still our beacon.

It took 14 years to complete the Mount Rushmore sculpture representing these four presidents who contributed so much to securing our freedom and growth as a nation. The state and federal governments have been instituted to secure the above unalienable rights, but what does this mean? This is where we start.

Politics used to be the art of compromise, or was it the art of horse trading and earmarking legislation, and now it is all about buying votes, raising campaign funds, and voting the party line. I didn't know America was for sale. Even the Continuing Resolution that reopened the government in 2013 year was loaded with earmarks. We need to sculpture a vision of how our government should function for us, Americans. A vision of how Congress and the President should carry out their Constitutional responsibilities for America, within American values.

American Values

American values differ for every American just as does the American dream. We discussed "The American Dream" earlier in this book where I tried to express what I thought it meant in so many words. Nowhere is this term, "The American Dream", used in the Declaration of Independence or the U.S. Constitution. However, in the book, *The Epic of America*, written by James Truslow Adams, Adams describes it as *"that dream of a land in which life should be better and richer and fuller for everyone, with opportunity for each according to ability or achievement. It is a difficult dream for the European upper classes to interpret adequately, and too many of us ourselves have grown weary and mistrustful of it. It is not a dream of motor cars and high wages merely, but a dream of social order in which each man and each woman shall be able to attain to the fullest stature of which they are innately capable, and be recognized by others for what they are, regardless of the fortuitous circumstances of birth or position."* What the American dream and American values have in common is how Americans want to live in our country, what has meaning to them with regard to life, liberty and happiness.

When the government goes too far or when it doesn't go far enough, when laws or public policy unfairly treat special interest over the common good, or when government or Congress allow for wasteful spending, unaccountability, and proliferation of government agencies it impacts our lives because we see unfairness, lawlessness, and we see we have less resources to provide the opportunities we value in America. We feel our tax money is being wasted and that the government is ineffective. The balance is delicate but not impossible. The government and Congress need to stop spending on other than national interests. Fix the issues mentioned in Chapter 2 with regard to the size of the government and fraud, waste and abuse. Deal with tax and regulation issues that are impacting economic growth.

Think simple, think focused on a common destiny, and think values that Americans deal with every day, like balancing their checkbooks. We are over thinking all of this thanks to politics. Take the politics out of governing this nation. It is like they say, when things seem overwhelming break it down into small tasks. Don't try to fix the entire tax code, just fix what is unfair to the individual tax system, such as a single flat tax, and lower the corporate tax rate. Don't pass complicated legislation loaded with special interest projects that do not serve the many, pass an appropriations bill that outlines what missions in the federal government need to be funded that represent what we value within Constitutional limits and what programs provide for social and economic growth. Once such legislation is passed it is Congress and the government's duty to oversee the funds allocated to protect against fraud, waste, and abuse. Enforce the laws already on the books or get rid of them. Defund agencies that cannot show value or duplicate missions with other agencies. Stop borrowing from "Peter to pay Paul". Have the work ethic to sort out what missions need to be adequately funded and which ones not, but no more lazy across the board funding cuts known as sequestration in the Budget Control Act.

There is lots of real work to be done. Even members of Congress want to work, after all they are Americans. Let the work begin. Consider and take on some reforms mentioned in Chapter 3 to allow for more partisanship and participation by all members of Congress that want the opportunity to discuss and consider legislation and not just follow the party line and party leadership. We elected people to Congress, not parties. Let them do their job and have a voice.

We have to get our house in order so we don't lose the real American dream and our right to life, liberty, and pursuit of happiness. If our house is not in order we lose our stance in the world. The following values need to guide us in measuring our success as a nation.

Opportunity

Americans want to work and they want jobs that have meaning to them and that pay a fair salary. Small business wants to grow and thrive. Our children want the opportunity to hone a skill or cure disease. The degree the government can remove the obstacles to opportunity for Americans will measure our success as a nation. The American dream is one of believing in hard work and hope, believing in what the future can hold, while holding our values close as we start the journey. It is about adversity and perseverance. It is about quality over quantity, pride in our efforts. It is about sharing the dream with other countryman and immigrants because that is what makes America unique. The degree to which private enterprise, serving as a conduit to this dream, take the risk to progress our people and our nation itself will be our measure.

The degree to which we build innovation and technology in our children's education and create opportunity in the form of jobs for Americans not to be sent overseas will be our measure. Apprenticeship programs and other training initiatives will be important to safeguard our children from going in the wrong direction. As mentioned in my Domestic Plan in Chapter 1, government and private enterprise need to collaborate to promote economic and technological growth and reduce our dependency on the government. According to officials at the Federal Election Commission, the 2012 presidential election cost 7 billion dollars. Just think what we could have achieved if we had put that money into public works. It is all turned upside down. Americans don't care about campaigns, they care even less about political parties. Let us get our priorities in order.

Remember the movie "The Pursuit of Happiness", starring Will Smith who plays in the tale inspired by the true story of Chris Gardner? In the movie Chris Gardner worked hard and suffered many obstacles but he persevered for his son and, thanks to an unpaid internship in a stockbroker-training program, he was able to see his dream come true. Internships and other collaborations between public and private organizations can tap into existing resources that can result in innovations beyond our imaginations creating a bridge for the next generation. The degree to which American business supports these type of programs will be our measure of American business commitment to the growth of opportunity in the U.S. I see success through collaboration, not competition, especially in the millennial or Y generation. Education costs need to be contained. They keep rising when incomes remain stagnant. Federal loans keep the money flowing to the colleges but this doesn't solve the cost problem. Something else needs to be done to contain costs.

Fairness and Responsibility

Taxes need to be simple and fair. No one wants to pay taxes but if you have income the tax should be fair based on amount of income. Corporate tax rates should be lowered more in line with other countries. The measure of success would be more jobs staying in the U.S. and more tax revenue to offset the deficit that we have been building. Free trade policy needs to be enforced so that U.S. goods can be sold overseas. We have had a trade deficit for over a decade. Moving American jobs overseas has furthered the deficit. Regulations impacting business need to be reviewed and changed if deemed unfair.

Enforcing laws and taking responsibility for wrong doing is part of the American backbone. Lawlessness as we have seen in the mortgage crisis goes against our grain as well as the government bailouts to corporations who defrauded Americans. Mortgage safeguards put in place following the Great Depression need to be put back in place. Executive actions have also contributed to the fear that the balance of power is being jeopardized. The executive branch policies should not be changed or ignored to circumvent the law.

Immigration policy needs to be enforced until it is changed by law. The open border (700 miles) needs to be secured and border security officials should be allowed to do their jobs. Those who follow the existing legal process to citizenship should not be displaced and sent to back of the line by those entering the country illegally. Allowing five million illegal immigrants amnesty to remain in the country is not fair to Americans seeking jobs and paying taxes that are being used to assist these illegal immigrants.

Federal agencies not focusing on their missions and overstepping their authority need to take responsibility including the IRS, EPA, and the Veterans Administration (VA) to name a few. Bogus bonuses should not be tolerated and officials should be fired for mismanagement. Regulators and the Fed Secretary need to do their jobs as well.

Government contracts need to be overseen properly by the government and overseen by Congress so they do not run over budget and over schedule or change the type of contracts used. This wrongdoing is measurable if the government and Congress impose their oversight responsibilities.

Responsible spending is what the public demands. Stop spending money on pork barrel projects, bridges to nowhere. Focus on national interests and on collaboration, combining existing programs and projects that are similar instead of duplication of missions and costs.

Freedom and Security

The national debt interferes with the U.S. ability to invest in the future and impacts our freedom and security. If the country had a surplus we could invest back into economic growth, jobs, college education for our children to meet the skills imbalance and high cost of education. Instead we pay interest to other countries that own a piece of America.

Morality, leadership for the free world, the duty to stand up for those repressed is an American value. Americans need to define the "red line" and the government needs to develop a strategy to concur terrorism. Cyber terrorism and other terrorism needs to be a top priority. Since we share many concerns with Europe and other nations, collaboration among the United Nations for the better of all might be a better approach to security, global warming, and assistance to our poorer nations. The rally in France was a strong sign of solidarity among world leaders. Sad that the U.S. was a no show.

We should not release criminals from prison just so they can go back and commit crimes in the U.S. and overseas that threaten our security. The morale of our military and border security officers that risk their lives to capture these criminals is negatively impacted. If the southern border and the northern border are not secured we risk criminals entering our country. We need to identify those who have already entered the country illegally and determine their status and educate them on the process toward citizenship.

Job security and retirement are concerns for many Americans. How we deal with these issues is a measure of our success as a nation. Now that businesses no longer offer pensions, something needs to be done to ensure money is saved for retirement. I am not convinced the 401(k) fund is the complete answer to a secure retirement for many.

General Welfare

I don't think that we need to go backwards in our support for social programs that fill the gap between low income families and middle class families. We have to oversee signs of fraud, waste, and abuse in these programs and make them financially sustainable. And, by the way, a lot of former middle class are now the recipients of these programs. Too many in America are going hungry. This in itself is a measure that we have to take action. How can the richest nation in the world have starving people? We have gone too far when individuals are arrested for feeding the homeless. It is all upside down.

The longer our elderly work, the less jobs will be available for other workers. If we cut federal programs or reorganize the government to be more efficient, the less federal government jobs will be available.

However, if investments are made by the federal government to improve our infrastructure with better bridges, roads, schools, renewable energy, education, scientific research, employment would increase and therefore additional tax revenue would be available.

I see welfare being a training ground or "bridge" for people who need work and new skills. Incentives to get off welfare should include making anyone on welfare work for the government while providing any necessary day care. This would also provide training and experience and require accountability for the benefits and give dignity to the experience.

Education reform and modernization could play a key role in eradicating all kinds of social problems. Teachers who are measured for performance and then paid or rewarded for that performance is essential and would be better spent than supporting bureaucratic school system administrations. I see higher education being more attainable to those who have great potential and to those who aspire to not only focus on the science, technology, engineering, and mathematics (STEM) career fields but also creativity, innovation, and collaboration. If we would seek out those with potential that may need a leg up with the cost of education, we would get way more back from the investment. You wouldn't need quotas for minorities at institutions of higher education if we focus on all those that are exceptional on an equal basis, the quota thing would fix itself.

Health care costs keep going up. Obamacare is not the answer. Mental health care access needs to be addressed. Proper care for our veterans needs to be fixed. What is the best way to solve these related problems? Expanding Medicare to those who needed health care might have been a better approach to Obamacare? What is the best system to care for our veterans? Is the VA the answer?

Paying it Forward

America is a giving country. Americans want to give but we need to give back more to Americans. I see the one percent wealthy donating much of their money for public good. I see "big business" paying it forward to their employees and their families. Taking their huge profits and making a difference in their employee's lives, returning to American values. This is a win-win situation, whether in the form of jobs, a pension or other types of benefits. I believe that increased job growth and an improved training and educational system will have a ripple effect on health and wellbeing, reducing crime, and reducing homelessness and hunger. Veterans make up a large segment of our homeless even though much progress has been made by the VA efforts to assist homeless veterans. The war on poverty has not been successful. We need to focus on effective ways to combat these social issues and our ability to do so will be our measure of the character of this nation.

Americans are hopeful people. If you give them a leg up I believe they will pay it forward for others. It makes us feel good and gives meaning to life. We can't expect the government to do it all. We as a nation need to help where we can with charities and foundations that can benefit those who need a leg up. Here are just a few examples.

The Ginn Academy in Cleveland, Ohio, established by Ted Ginn Sr., is just one example of a high school alternative to public school and changing the lives of many boys every year, including Cardale Jones, the Ohio State University third string quarter back who led the Ohio State University to the 2014 football championship. There are many more good programs that private Americans have created to provide opportunity to our youth and adults.

Another example is helping our veterans using private donations to the National Wounded Warrior Center in Mammoth Lakes, California. This facility will enable Wounded Warriors to learn, heal, and give new meaning to their lives.

One Bistro is a community café that began in Miamisburg, Ohio, a suburb of Dayton, Ohio, that provides affordable meals to those who may not be able to pay, such as the homeless. According to the Xenia Gazette, "Meals range from $6-9, but One Bistro offers creative payment options. People who eat at One Bistro can pay only what they can afford;

pay the full amount or give extra to "pay it forward" to help feed someone else, or pay through service."

And then there is James Robertson, of Detroit, Michigan, a 56 year old factory worker who has walked a total of 21 miles to and from work for 10 years because his car broke down and he couldn't afford to buy a car. According to an article written by Bill Laitner, Detroit Free Press, "every trip is an ordeal of mental and physical toughness for this softspoken man with a perfect attendance record at work. And every day is a tribute to how much he cares about his job, his boss and his coworkers. Robertson's daunting walks and bus rides, in all kinds of weather…"

The story goes that after reading about the struggles of Mr. Robertson in the Detroit Free Press, Evan Leedy, a college student at Wayne State University created a Go Fund Me account on the internet to raise money to buy Mr. Robertson a car. There were two other Go Fund Me pages created by others for Mr. Robertson. Now all three fundraisers are working together and in only 3 days over $250,000 had been donated and more since then, including a new car donation by Honda. It wouldn't surprise me if Mr. Robertson pays a few things forward himself. The sky is the limit when we work together for a common cause.

Rev. Dr. Martin Luther King, Jr., in his speech on August 28, 1963, on the steps of the Lincoln Memorial during the march on Washington for

Jobs and Freedom, was famous for expressing his dream that his children would be able to live in a nation that would not judge them by the color of their skin but by the content of their character. He was so right. And so it goes that the character of our people will reflect the character of our nation. So let's keep moving forward focusing on character and American values.

ABOUT THE AUTHOR

Nancy Elshoff Parks spent 36 years as a government public servant. She worked three years as a legislative analyst, subcommittee staffer, and bill drafter for the West Virginia Legislature in the late 1970s. In 1980, she went to work for the federal government as a program analyst. She retired in 2014, after 33 years of federal government service. She has a degree in Political Science from the University of Cincinnati. She knows how the federal government works from having worked in the government. She understands the legislative process as well. She writes this book as an American citizen concerned about the future of our nation and the futures of our children and grandchildren. She sets out to understand the political and economic policy situations that have impacted the middle and lower classes of Americans as they struggle to rebound from decades of money and power games over our government officials and policies. She analyzes many of our political and economic problems and provides specific recommendations on how to fix many of the problems in hopes of providing a guiding light into the future of America. She has lived most of her life in Ohio. She is married to her husband Dan and has a son, Mason, and two step daughters, Bridget and Andrea, and two step grandchildren, Thomas and Victoria.

www.ingramcontent.com/pod-product-compliance
Lightning Source LLC
Chambersburg PA
CBHW030758180526
45163CB00003B/1071